C000002699

PROLOGUE

July 1913

Eugène Christophe

What passes through your mind when you're riding? If you're any good… nothing.

You are man become machine, finely tuned and focused on race and race alone.

Entire towns line the streets to watch this man become machine for what, a second or two, and they go back to their grubby homes to dream of life on the road, of being you, that person on the back of a cigarette card, but who are you really? Where are you at any one moment?

You start in one town; you end up in another. You start with one regional dialect, and end up with another language entirely. It doesn't matter that the people round here speak some unintelligible patois, the man become machine is gone in a flash. Bye bye, adios, au revoir, I wish I could stick around.

The world around you passes by in a blur, forever changing from town square to cathedral to field to hillock, and if you stop to think about it, you've lost. So you pedal, and you find your rhythm, man becomes machine so legs become pistons, belly becomes fire pit, food is your coal and you shovel it in.

And then you stop.

The wheels come off, the tyre blows or the forks break and you snap out of that racing trance. One minute you're racing, the next you're a man with a broken bike. Man and machine separated, and for a split second you're in between, working out what's happened, what's gone wrong, why has the factory stopped producing?

And this is me.

Thys the Belgian has made good for Luchon, I'm sure of it. He'll be halfway down the mountain by now and he won't know until he reaches his hotel bedroom tonight that Christophe has blown his chances of winning the Tour. He'll be looking over his shoulder fearing the Frenchman, not knowing that he's out of the Tour or at best, out of contention.

It happened at the top of the Tourmalet. I'd taken the Osquich partly by foot, to save energy for the three main climbs of the day, the Tourmalet, the Aspin and the Peyresourde. These are not roads, these are goat paths, so when there is energy to be saved, you save it, even if Henri Desgrange will mock you for dismounting in tomorrow's paper.

I'd started my descent when the front wheel started to float in between the forks. That split second seemed to last forever. Man wrenched from machine, and the sudden realisation that the ravine to my left was inching closer. Not now, I pleaded. Not here. Not her.

In these parts, a witch preys upon cyclists. They say she has green teeth, and there are rumours she has cousins, sisters, evil twins cast around the cycling world, ready to strike a cyclist down for hunger, ill luck, mechanicals. One in the Alps. One in the Arenberg Forest near Roubaix. And one here, in the Pyrenees. She found me here, at the top of the Tourmalet, at the top of my form, and she turned my whole world upside down in a split second that nearly never ended.

I tensed every muscle. I clenched the cold steel of the brakes and held myself straight. The smell of burning rubber a sign that I was alive, the fractured forks a sign that my race was not. The forks were broken at the support; a mechanic as skilled as I would quickly know that this was not a fracture that could be patched up and ridden to the finish, this was the end of the bike as we know it.

And the first realisation I was losing the race came when someone – was it Defraeye – came past, screaming at me to get out of the way. Others – Alavoine, Lambot, Garrigou – the whole field in the end, taking the hairpins down the Tourmalet shouting abuse, some shouting commiserations, some barely noticing me.

What were they thinking? They were good, so nothing.

I picked the bike up and started walking.

With every step, a decision to make. Do I give in? Do I get in the car that I know is following 50 steps behind? Do I carry on down the Tourmalet on foot, in the hope that somewhere there's a smithy with a forge hot enough to repair this fork?

Of course I carry on. In the words of my father, you never leave a job half done.

And with every step down, extra weight. With every footstep, a further dig into my shoulder.

And worse, with each footstep, thoughts. None of the clarity that comes with bike racing, just the muddle that ordinary people have to put up with every day. What do you think of when you're walking down a mountain?

Everything, that's what. So down the mountain I go, alone but for the commissaire's car and the sounds of the mountain. The heat is burning mud into flakes that shatter with every footstep. Who knows, by the time I reach a blacksmith's, I may be clean.

The Tourmalet. Round here, it means wrong turn. Others don't bother learning the local dialect, but I do - you never know when it might come in handy. Tour-mal-et. It's all taken a wrong turn. And it's all so quiet. Above me, only sky. Below me, half the world. A craggy green carpet that stretches down in folds and bumps.

I replay the moment – why not. The trance is gone, and what else can you do? You think that by replaying the moment in your mind that maybe it will resolve itself differently. The moment the wheel started to rattle itself loose of the sprocket, in another reality, that may not have happened. The moment the fork shattered, it may - in another world - have just cracked, and I might have made it down the Tourmalet on two wheels, not on two feet. In another reality, Eugène Christophe has caught up with Philippe Thys, he's overhauled him, he's racing with the wind behind his back, he's crossing the line in Luchon.

Or I may have lost control entirely and ended up down the ravine.

The bike's getting heavier. I pour the remaining water from one of the bidons over my head, and for a second or two I feel an intense pleasure before crashing back to earth and the Tourmalet and the pain and the sweat. And I look around.

It's beautiful in this part of the world. I know it's a beast of a climb, but we should come here more often than just once a year. They make us race in the north so often, a land so grey and flat it surprises me they turn out such beasts of men so frequently, beasts who bike everywhere it's as if they were born on wheels. Once these men discovered the velocipede they were off - find me new lands, they'd say, take me far from here, until they discovered the velocipede was hard work, and you'd only get as far as the next town. They then discovered even the next town was as dark and foreboding as the last one. And so they got stronger and they got stronger still. You have men like Scieur, Defraeye, Lambot - proper, true, stoic men with hearts of gold and lungs of charcoal, solid men of the north whose one ambition is to keep moving, keep racing so you don't see the darkness of the landscape and you don't feel the harshness of the cobblestones beneath your wheels.

And men like Lambot come here, in this sea of bright green and rock, and they ride head down, legs pumping like pistons in a Walloon factory, in their racing trance. When they get home to their wives who ask - where did you go today my sweetheart, they say - I don't know, my dear, but I ended up somewhere adequate.

So the Tourmalet, I suppose, is my prize. I may have lost the Tour, and I may have wasted the last three weeks of my life, but I win the Tourmalet, and I get to carry my cross down to whichever small town happens to have a blacksmith's. A forge in which to repair this crocked Peugeot. I'll have lost, but you never leave a job half done.

What to do, then. A song, maybe? To keep me from crying. Or laughing.

At last, signs of life. How long have I been walking? An hour? Three hours? You can hardly tell. There's that summer silence you get up here, a warm stillness broken by the sound of wasps. The sign says Sainte-Marie de Campan and like most of these towns, the Tour is what happens to the cities. A bike race, you say? Well, I'd heard they do that, in the cities. A bike race, indeed.

A girl, probably 10 or 11 years old, in a field of goats. Its cliché, but she's wearing a gingham dress and a straw hat.

See what I mean? You stop cycling; the world lays itself out in front of you.

"Young girl, is there a blacksmith's in this town"

"De que?"

Neither French nor Spanish... I had never stopped in these parts before.

"A blacksmith. Broken bike. Repair."

If in doubt, point and shout. I bet she's never met a locksmith from Malakoff before. But some French comes back.

"Try Elie Bède, he owns the sawmill in town. He should be able to help you."

A sawmill. It might be all I need, if he has the tools.

I cross the town square, my heart pumping. Can anyone save this bike? I knock on the door marked "Bède".

A bald man, clearly still digesting his food, takes a step out of the door to take a look at the Peugeot.

"Eh fuck," he chuckles. "You've got work to do."

"So can you help? Do you have tools?"

He takes a closer look, craning his neck. "Ahh... you see, I can weld small things here and there, but round tubes like that, no. You'll need Joseph Bayle – he's our blacksmith. He's got the fire you want."

"So where will I find this Bayle?"

He gives me a look as if to say "wait there", and turns his head inside the door. "Hey, Maria. Take this man to Bayle, will you?"

I follow Maria up the road to the church, and then back down the steepest of cobbled roads. I lose my footing twice, the bike nearly losing my shoulder. On another day, I would have admired Maria. The curve of her legs, the simple skirt, the high shoulders.

Not today. When will this end? Maria turns another corner. How big is this town meant to be? Too many questions.

Finally, on the edges of town, a thatched roof cottage and a wrought iron sign that modestly states "Bayle, 1900". A column of smoke rises from the chimney. A smoke signal. A forge.

"Joseph!" cries Maria. "Joseph, open up, there's a stranger here for you!"

The battle-ridden face of Joseph Bayle appears, covered in soot, followed quickly by those of his wife and two daughters at the window.

"Good God, what have we here?"

We've been here before.

"My bike broke, and I'm in rather a hurry."

He looks the bike up and down, and then looks me up and down.

"So you're one of those Tour de France men, that right?"

"That's right. So can you help?"

He pulls the tradesman face. "Well it's that… you see, I've never repaired a bike. You should go ask Elie Bède, he knows how to do it."

"I did. His forge can't reach the 1,000 degrees I need. I'll need a round iron tube – 22 mm if you've got it."

Bayle nods and scurries off to find the tube, while the race commissaires explain my situation to Bayle's family. No help, I hear Baugé repeating. Nobody can help him. If anyone lifts so much as a finger to help him repair the bike, he'll be disqualified, or at best penalised.

A rage rises up in me. All this time, they've followed me down the mountain, they've watched me suffer, they've seen me near collapse, in tears, and worse. Singing.

And here's Mousset, the worst of the race commissaires, a face that has seen foie gras and Sauternes sweet wine.

A face that has sat in front of many log fires, with fat, pudgy hands that stroke his moustache, this triple-chinned layabout who dares to throw the rulebook at me in this hour. Who does the witch think she is, sending me Mousset? That repulsive human.

"On his own? Are you mad!" shouts Bayle, genuinely outraged on my behalf. "No man can repair a bike on his own, it takes two."

"Impossible," retorts Mousset with enormous pride. "If you give him any help whatsoever, the number 11 from the Peugeot team will be heavily penalised."

Baugé now: "Edmond. Can you not just avert your eyes for two seconds? Just while Monsieur Bayle operates the bellows?"

"I didn't write the rules, Alphonse," he retorts, pulling at his lapels. He's breaking into a sweat now. The fire is reaching the heat I require.

"And make sure you don't just replace the part. You must repair it, not replace it."

To work, then. To work, the work that sustained me before the racing, and will likely sustain me afterwards. To work, the locksmith turned cyclist turned mechanic.

It is 3 o'clock. Thys will be on the podium with Garrigou, maybe Defraeye. I bury myself in the task, hammering and knocking, beating the iron, hurling with the rage and the fury built up from the peace of the Tourmalet, and with each blow of the hammer, the mercury rises further. Mousset pulls at his collar, Baugé shuffles uncomfortably, Bayle looks on with pride. I have never been more at home.

To work, then. Never leave a job half done. I remind myself that when I'm done with cycling, this is all I'll have.

There's a changing of the guard behind me. Baugé, no doubt, has gone to celebrate Thys' victory. Dugand is here, Cazalis too, funereal faces all. Mousset has had enough, so Steinbach has replaced him. Who would have thought that so many would come to watch my downfall, here in Sainte-Marie de Campan? I look at Bayle's face, a picture of admiring concentration, and I realise that for Bayle, today is not my downfall, it is the making of me. For what more of me would he know, other than my ability to repair this rotten bike?

From the jaws of defeat, victory – if not the victory I was seeking, victory all the same.

"Is there any chance of a sandwich?" murmurs Lecomte, who has appeared as if from nowhere.

A switch inside me has flipped. I turn and summon all my fury from the pits of my own personal hell, and project towards the commissaire.

"Eat coal. I'm your prisoner, and if this is a prison, you'll do as I do and you'll eat when I'm done."

Bayle nods appreciatively, and silence falls.

To work, then. It doesn't fit, so I remove the rod and file down, I keep filing and filing, hammering and hammering, filing further until the iron rod enters. I hammer, I push. The rod, smooth as silk, slips in like it had always been there. And it had.

But one task remained. The bellows. How can I operate the bellows and hold the forks myself? The hope and the pride of the last hour's work dissipates immediately.

"Can't you see," I hear Bayle pleading at whichever commissaires remain behind me, "he needs help. It's a small job. Come on."

"Article 45, paragraph 2, the rules clearly state that the rider must repair it by his own hands, and his own hands alone."

Desmarets is speaking now. Where do they all come from? He's arguing my case. Lecomte is arguing against it.

But what if… what if a child operated the bellows? Surely they can't stop a child.

There's a boy who has been watching behind Joseph Bayle all this time. I summon him over. Hand him the bellows. Here, young man, don't feel guilty if they penalise me, all you have to do is blow, blow gently with these bellows. Here, take this. Don't look at them, look at me, that's right, just look at me. And blow. Gently. Don't be afraid.

I stand back and admire my work. Bayle too. I may have lost the Tour today, but I've won something else. Something more grand than the Tour. Right here, in Joseph Bayle's forge in Sainte-Marie de Campan, I've won. I've beaten the witch. I've beaten Desgrange. I've shown Baugé that you don't have to cross the line first to win a race.

You just have to choose your race.

10 pm

I lost four hours today; or was it five or three. I don't know. It barely matters.

I lost the Tour, most of all. I lie here, caked in dust, tyres fused into my jersey from the heat in Bayle's forge. From the black of the afternoon to the white of the night. I watch the curtains dance, and I'm reminded of Maria's skirt.

I lie here, the centre of attention, the dogs at my door. I ignore the knocks. Someone calls, I shout "piss off" and chuckle to myself. Thys and Petit-Breton will be seething. To them, the spoils; to me, the victory. Bittersweet, true. But a victory nonetheless.

I hear Desgrange in the corridor, and I can see him now – chest out, moustache twirled – arm round the disconsolate winner. Our Tour's organiser, organising the lives and the stories that sell his newspaper every day. The Tour is his life; he lives and breathes this bike race, and he feels every pothole, every bump in the road. This is his moment as much as mine. He'll have filed his story, his heroic epic for tomorrow's yellow rag, and he'll be counting the cash.

Eugène Christophe, hero of the Tourmalet. He won all our hearts, but he won't win the race.

November 1918 - Armistice Day

Henri Desgrange

Alphonse Baugé raises his glass, swallows another glass of my cheapest red, and continues to lay obstacles in my path.

"Henri, this Tour cannot take place, only a lunatic would stage a bike race in these conditions."

The man is a fool. It's a shame, for once he was a fine cyclist, albeit a cyclist without any significant victories but alas... For every winner, there are a hundred losers.

However, as a trainer, 'Marshall Baugé' came into his own, moulding the late, dearly missed François Faber into quite the rider and quite the man. The kind of man who would carry his own dead comrades back from no man's land and take a bullet for the cause himself.

Baugé can be proud of that. And Peugeot could be proud of the man they plucked from amateur obscurity. For every hundred Baugé-the-cyclists, there is just one Baugé-the-trainer.

But today, Baugé is an idiot throwing thumbtacks into the wheels of progress. A fly in my ointment.

"Listen, Alphonse," and this is more emollience on my behalf, you will hear plenty of it. "France is hurting. We are hurting. And I can tell that without François, you are hurting too. The countryside is devastated, we have lost how many men, I don't know, far too many for my liking, and yet we must play our part in strengthening the bonds between our people - they will need spectacle, they will need rousing from their stupor, they will need heroes."

Ah, I give a good speech.

Here he goes… he's going to count on his fingers. Every gesture Alphonse makes is prepared several seconds in advance.

"Manufacturing, Henri - a simple matter, really. How many tyres do you think we can manufacture? The factories have been closed, bombed, or requisitioned. On these roads, the riders will puncture every 200 metres if they are lucky. I simply cannot provide this level of support."

He can. He will. Next.

"And the bike manufacturers, Henri - Peugeot cannot put out a team, I can tell you that for a fact - Alcyon barely exists, Delage might not be able to put another bike together and JB Louvet's factory needs significant repairs if they are to start production again."

I have a plan, Alphonse, but do carry on; I see your third finger is already prepared.

"The riders - are they demobilised? Are they fit? How can you expect anyone to take this route you're suggesting? 5,500 km across 15 stages? It's your most ridiculous plan yet, even in normal conditions. The riders will need months of preparation, and I'd be willing to wager that none of them would have any more than a few weeks at most."

Oh, and the war-shy Henri Pélissier has been fighting the Boche with his bare hands, has he? Alphonse knows very well that half the riders have been riding for two years whenever they pleased, and there are other races that will no doubt go ahead before this, giving them the chance to reach peak fitness by July. But here comes finger number four.

"And do you seriously propose to force these men to ride over bomb craters, half-destroyed cobblestones, through our once-proud, torn-apart towns… men who have barely recovered from the war effort, men who have seen their comrades die, men whose fellow cyclists are dead. You're going to make them ride through towns like Amiens, for Christ's sake. Amiens!"

Easy with the wine, Alphonse. No more fingers, I notice.

Emollience. I'll stand for this one, although at my age… yes, I'll stand.

"Alphonse, dear boy." I walk around the back of his chair and massage his shoulders. Skin and bones, our Alphonse, underneath that cheap suit. "Alphonse, Alphonse. I have a plan. The genesis of a plan, but do hear me out.

"I understand your worries, and yes - I share them, truly I do. But the need to lift this nation weighs far too heavily upon my shoulders not to respond to this calling, and you too must respond to it, Alphonse. You too must heed the call and fight this new fight, and I will help you. I have spoken already with Louvet, Hutchison, Alcyon and Automoto, they have all agreed to participate in whichever way they can, so how's about this…"

Oh, Alphonse, did you not see this coming? I'll take a seat for this bit.

"We have one team. Let's call it La Sportive for now. All professional riders from previously professional teams will ride under the banner of one team - that's anyone with an A licence - they will be riding for you, and you will all have the opportunity to promote your cyclists and your machines as you wish, but you are one, single, indivisible entity."

"Henri," he splutters, "that's…"

"Genius?"

"It's fucking ridiculous!"

"I'm glad you like it. L'Auto will plan the routes extremely carefully, we will make sure to avoid the most heavily cratered areas, but it is highly important that our course take in the areas most affected by this awful, awful war. For the people of those regions, so that we never forget. We will go to Alsace, we will pass through Lorraine…"

"But they're still bloody Germans!" Alphonse nearly explodes at this. "You can't expect to receive a hero's welcome everywhere you go, Henri."

"They're not Germans any more, Alphonse, they're French. This Tour will be for them and they'll be reminded that in our eyes, they always have been French. And they will welcome our riders as their own. Heroes. French men. And some Belgians and maybe an Italian or two if we can convince Girardengo to race."

Alphonse slumps into his chair and sniffs lazily at the cheap plonk. His resistance is waning. It's a shame, because I was beginning to get into my stride.

Desmarets, who has been asleep throughout the whole conversation, is beginning to stir.

"Ah, Robert, you're back in the land of the living, how nice of you to rejoin us."

"I was just resting my eyes," he lies.

Desmarets, my useful idiot. Young, impetuous, baby-faced, but best of all an absolute arse-licker. And a half-decent journalist, when he tries.

"Not to worry, Bob, I was just explaining to our friend

Alphonse here that he will be leading the team La Sportive during the Tour de France next summer. A collective of all of France's finest bicycle manufacturers, riding together under one banner. Naturally, the finer details will have to be ironed out - I would suggest a rationing of tyres, a pooling of soigneurs, and we at L'Auto would have to give serious consideration to using army barracks wherever possible instead of hotels, but Alphonse, you need not worry yourself over these finer details, relax, dear Alphonse, relax. Drink some more wine."

Desmarets can't stop himself. "Did you tell him about Metz-Dunkirk?"

Alphonse is practically straining at the leash here. Sorry, old boy. Yes, I have already designed the route - I've been designing the route in my head for the last five years of this wretched war, I've been plotting every column inch, writing every word for every stage. I dare say I've even chosen the winner.

For every cyclist who died in the war, I will stage this Tour. For François Faber, for Octave Lapize, for Lucien Petit-Breton - men who could have won this race, do you think they would have wanted us to bend over and submit to the will of the Boche long after they've been cleansed from our lands? I will stage this Tour. Do you think that a few craters or a couple of recently demobilised riders would get in my way? Everyone wants the Tour, and nobody wants it more than me, so no, I have not told him about Metz-Dunkirk. I have not told him about Geneva, the Galibier, the Aspin and the Peyresourde. I have not told him that in one single day they'll be riding 450 km, and I haven't told him we plan to end one stage in the violent, stinking hell hole that is Marseille. I will stage this Tour.

Alphonse doesn't need to know all of this.

"Alphonse, we'll clarify the route over the next few months, but I'm asking you now, dear boy, as this race is very much taking place, and it is very much going to be a success, would you be part of it?"

"You're a madman, Desgrange."

"Yes, Alphonse. I'm afraid I rather am."

11pm

It is rather late. Alphonse and Desmarets have long since gone, and the embers of the fire are spitting their last. I am well aware of the practicalities of organising this Tour, well aware of the difficulties. The Germans will have signed the Armistice by now; they'll be clearing the trenches as we speak. But what led us to this?

I'll tell you. It's indolence. Oh, I was just five years old when the Prussians besieged Paris, but I remember it as if it were yesterday, my mother sheltering me as the earth shook and the plaster fell from the ceiling. I remember the hunger, there were children wandering the streets, hunting for rats, and there were rumours that children would be on the menu if no rats could be found. We were born from war, and why were we so humiliated? Indolence.

Our nation had grown fat. Lazy. Men were incomparable to the filthy Boche, they were more interested in smoking, or lazing around in bars drinking themselves stupid. The Boche were lean, fit and could fight all day. Our men? Fat or foppish; no match for the wretched krauts.

Men need sport. Without sport, without sporting heroes, without the sacrifice of athletes pushing themselves to the very limits of human potential, man grows indolent. It was indolence that lost us the war in 1871. We shall never return to those days, at least not under my watch. And if we have suffered for the last four years, we need to make sure there is no repeat of this suffering.

Men need men. Inspirational examples of what man can be.

What better example can there be than the great Eugène Christophe, carrying his bike down the mountain in 1913, to repair the bike by his own hands in Sainte-Marie de Campan. A man whose very own motto is you never leave a job half done. Christophe, the old Gaul, the tradesman who never gives up, who never says "I can't do this", what better example of a man can there be? Or the Italian Girardengo, il Campionissimo, the finest cyclist Italy ever did produce, a thin, wiry, man of exemplary behaviour and courtesy, punching his way through the mountains. Should the Tour attract Costante… ah… what a Tour it would be.

So when the men of today and the men of tomorrow gather by the roadside in July, they will do so to admire the feats of our thoroughbred athletes, and they will be so inspired at the pain and the suffering these men experience in their daily toil, that they will never again fall into indolence, even if merely out of shame for their own fecklessness. The Tour leads by example and if at any point I am accused of working my riders to the bone, I will reply - aye, that may be your interpretation, but this rider is twenty times the man you will ever be, and he is doing this for you, for your own good, for the love of country. Be ashamed that you cannot equal the feats of this locksmith, or God forbid, an Italian.

I will stage this Tour, dear reader. Just you watch me.

STAGE 1
PARIS TO LE HAVRE

Firmin Lambot

I... am... not... going... to... make... it...

Ah fuck. No. A shower of mud from Van Daele's back wheel sprays me direct in the face, my goggles are covered – ah fuck, I can't see, shit I'm going down. Who's that in the way now? How can I know – but he's holding me up. Let me go down, bastard. Let me fall.

Bastard. Shit. Fuck.

Mud tastes the same all over France, by the way. In case you were wondering.

Ah Jesus, this is pain like I've never known it. Shit, another pothole, the bike nearly somersaults. I still can't see.

"Stay straight you fucking Belgian", shouts someone French.

"Allez Déjo", shouts a friendlier voice, definitely Léon. I might not have my eyes, but I have my ears.

He has his hand around me, so I can at least wipe my goggles and work out where I am. It's chaos. Mud, shit flying everywhere, rain battering you from the side, headlamps lighting up the raindrops in the interminable grey – the never-ending fucking grey, and the sound of men shouting, most of them in pain.

My legs, I'm not fit. I'm not ready. I can't go on.

I clench my teeth, where's Van Daele's wheel gone? He's a good one to hang on to. Broad-shouldered and steady. Nobody likes a wheelsucker, but what choice do I have?

"Déjo, relax," Léon hollers from two back, "remember your training!"

Ah now yes, thanks Léon, I do remember my fucking training. I vomited every day for the first week climbing the Côte de Goschenée over and over again, my head was burning with the effort, but how would you be after four years off the bike, eating the scraps the krauts left behind?

This is a party in comparison. So suck it up, Firmin, ride on. Find that wheel and suck it.

Spit out the grit.

The buildings are shooting up now; where five minutes ago we passed farmsteads and half-dead villages, this is clearly a town, but what hell is this? It must be Amiens. Oh boy. A handful of riders up front – Pélissier's among them – they hit the pedals hard. I don't remember any time bonuses up for grabs here, that would be some sad fucking joke to award bonuses for coming through here first. The only reason for sprinting here would be to get through it as quickly as you can.

I saw Leuven and what the Germans had done to the library and the town centre – and that sticks with you. It sticks in your gut and it burns and the taste never leaves you, but Amiens. What have those bastards done? Most of the peloton slows down and gape. The Cathedral – God save them – what were they thinking?

"Head down, Firmin." It's Léon again, my guardian

Belgian. "Watch your wheel mate, we don't need to see this."

"But look at the people, Paupou – look at their faces."

"Don't look up Firmin, just ride. Fight the pain, but don't look up."

Tommies line the street, a four-year war etched on their faces like twenty years of torture, and they're screaming for us. Women – women everywhere – a hundred times stronger than they ever were, working women, women who are doing men's jobs, women who've grown their hair short and are wearing suits – just women, bellowing their support in the shadows of the ruins. What is this insanity? Why us?

"Jesus wept," murmurs Léon as he freewheels through the cobbled streets.

Last year, we were tearing each other apart. What man can do to man, I still cannot comprehend. We'll never comprehend it. And now we're riding bikes through the rotting remains of the carnage, and all I can see is the gaps in peoples' teeth, like gaps in the buildings.

Everything used to be here.

Past Amiens, we pick up the speed and space out a little. Time for some in the peloton to stop for relief. A couple of guys find a café and dash inside. I think about it, but think better of it. And regret the decision, but you can't turn back.

Why did I choose this race? Why did I let Léon talk me into it? I could have sat it out, like so many did. Only 67 of us made it to the start line, whereas over 120 over-ambitious riders queued up at l'Auto's offices yesterday to sign up for the race. I bet only 20 of us will start tomorrow.

Thys pulls alongside. I never liked Thys. That chiselled face, the smooth demeanour, that confidence. Some riders·win races and some riders, like Thys, feel like they own them.

"How much are they paying you, Déjo?"

I tut. It's always money with Thys.

"Same as you, I guess."

He tuts. We could tut all the way to Paris.

"Don't you think you're worth more? You won the mountains last time, Firmin. You should ask for more money."

I nudge a wheel ahead of him. Cyclist-speak for "I'm done". He nudges alongside.

"I told Desgrange," he goes on. "I told him – I won this for you last time, I'm your star man, pay me properly or I walk. That's what I said; you know what he said? You know what he said? You're no more important than Nempon to me. Nempon! That peasant boy with a B-licence."

He's still talking. "All this A-licence nonsense. Grey shirts, hardly any supplies, I reckon this is the bike I rode the 1913 Tour on. What a load of rubbish, Déjo. And for what? Huh?"

I nod. I've heard this before from Thys. I look down at his back wheel.

"46 x 19 is that? Should have gone with 21 today."

A look of thunder. I ride on. I might not win this stage, or this Tour, but I've won that conversation.

Next stop Abbeville for a checkpoint and food. I've still got two baguettes left in my back pockets. I take one out – cheese, I reckon – cheese and mud with a casing of grit. I lick the baguette and spit out the flecks of muck. Some of the spit hits an Italian lad who's panting like a dog to my left.

I pull over underneath an awning and pull out the stage route as the rain pounds on the shelter above me. Huge thick droplets are pouring off.

I yank out the route map. From here, it's a windy, sinuous

route to the coast at Le Tréport, where there's another checkpoint. If I remember rightly, Le Tréport is the town with the coloured buildings, and a long, flat promenade, built for buffeting cyclists with sidewinds. Thys rolls past, glaring at me, glaring at everyone. You get the feeling he's spoiling for a fight.

At this rate, neither of us will reach the mountains. Henri Desgrange's shitshow has to go on, though. The only question is, will anyone make it?

Jean Alavoine

Jean Alavoine, I must say - you look amazing.

Why, thank you Jean Alavoine.

You're welcome, Jean Alavoine. And please, who do you think will win this Tour de France, Jean Alavoine?

Well, Jean Alavoine, I do believe Jean Alavoine has a flying chance, but in all seriousness, I'd be surprised if anyone makes it to Le Havre tonight.

Why do you say that, Jean Alavoine?

Have you seen the fucking roads? You'd have to be mental to ride your bike on these surfaces.

Anyway, Jean Alavoine, thanks for your time, and have a great nap.

Thanks, Jean Alavoine - oh, and tell that driver not to forget to wake me up in 20 minutes, will you?

This ditch has to be the most comfortable ditch in the north of France. A ditch fit for kings, you might say. To my left, a clump of grass that acts as a fine pillow, to my right, a small undulation that fits neatly with the small of my back. There's a few weeds that act as a canopy to take the edge off the rain, and time for a bit of shut-eye.

How did we get here? Let me take you back.

We left Paris at 2 in the morning, to the usual fanfare. Funny how people come out to watch people cycle away from them in the darkness, but there you go. The Tour de France - it's been away for 5 years and we're all pretending nothing happened in between by riding impossible bike races, and people in the cities spend their time watching impossible bike races, slapping us on the backs like we're heroes.

How many of us left this morning? I guess around 60 or 70, probably about half the number that turned up on the Boulevard Montmartre at l'Auto's offices to have our bikes stamped and our photos taken like convicts. 70 of us lined up, shivering in the dark, most of us wearing standard-issue grey shirts.

There isn't a race that doesn't start in the dark. That's how stupid bike racing is. One day, they'll look back at our generation and they'll laugh at us. The fools, riding like slaves all day and all night. There will be stages of 200 km, no more, and riders will be treated like kings. I tell you, one day this will happen.

Now, riding in the dark. The trick is to keep as close to the cars as possible, so you can read the roads. If you're at the back of the peloton, you're relying on reflections and moonlight. That's when you make mistakes. Stay close to the cars, stay close to each other, and stay away from the Pélissiers, because they're a pair of priggish tosspots. Especially Henri, my velodrome rival.

You're probably wondering how many punctures we've had? Oh yes, we have had plenty. Myself, I've had two. That means I've got two tyres left around my shoulders, kindly provided by Monsieur Baugé and the Sportive team. The bike manufacturers are all broke, of course, poor as dormice they are, so they've pooled together and we're all riding on the same team this year - yes, it's true, we're one big happy family now. And they give us four spare inner tubes a day. Any more than four punctures and you've got to either buy some more (keep your receipts, fellas) or rip out the lining and repair it yourself by the roadside. Oh, and don't ask for any help.

Some of the lads here raced the Tour of the Battlefields back in spring – now that was a race, by all accounts. Half of them abandoned halfway through the first stage, wheels buckled, tyres shredded, sod that for a game of soldiers. Stones, rubble, flint, potholes, cobblestones, bomb craters - you name it - they went through it and half of them didn't come out of it.

Deruyter won that race; now there's a man who can stay on his bike.

Nobody attacked on this stage until the sun rose, some massive Belgian lad who is probably on his way home as we speak, just take a right turn at Amiens and you're done, son. You've got your name in l'Auto and a contract when everything's back to normal. He'd have got his 5 franc bonus from the local café – now that's what I call a strategy. Stick around and you'll be racking up the bonuses on this Tour.

Trouble is, when the sun rises, you see the mess the Germans left behind. Dead trees, shelled roads, dead animals, burnt-out houses, flattened houses. As if we need reminding.

Eugène attacked as well, but we pulled him back in quickly enough. I thought I'd have a go and what do you know – I had nothing in the legs. Nothing at all. It would have been embarrassing, but nobody even noticed.

I lost touch when Henri Pélissier, Masson and Rossius got away. Sometimes, you have to withdraw. Live to fight another day.

Back to my ditch, then.

That driver's kicking me in the rump.

"Oi, Jean-boy, time to go."

That was a proper kick, too. "Alright, alright, Jesus. Room service in this ditch is terrible."

"You've lost 20 minutes, you know,"

"Ah yes, 20 minutes - I'll make them up later. Best 20 minutes' kip I've ever had. Thanks, son."

Where am I? Somewhere after Dieppe, I'd figure. Houses look different, Etretat, maybe? There's cliffs to my right and a town in the distance, maybe Fécamp. I'm entirely alone. I could do a Garin and catch the train, who would know?

So on I ride. Alone. This is what I remember from the Tours of old. The loneliness. You would spend several hours in the dark, pedalling in formation while some numbskull rides off thinking he can attack, and returns with his tail between his legs because he can't see without the headlamps of Desgrange's car. So it's a neutralised race and you're all friends, happy and chatty like women sewing. Ho ho, sun's up, off we go, and everyone's hunting bonuses like they're going out of fashion.

And then you're riding all day, sometimes in a group, but usually on your own. Nobody bothers watching you outside the towns and cities; maybe if you're lucky a dog will cross the road and take an interest.

Riding is lonely.

For some riders – no, forget that – for most riders, riding alone is the only way. I can't do that. I need to talk; I need company. Get me a peloton, and I'm your man.

It could be worse. You could be stuck with Henri Pélissier all day.

Henri Pélissier

Time to race! Time to show the world what Henri Pélissier is made of.

We're in Fécamp, so not far to go now, and at the checkpoint, it seems Christophe and Van Daele have got four minutes on us. Four minutes. Stop smelling the sea air and move it.

"Hey, Belgians," I shout out to my two spares, Scieur and Rossius, "they've got four minutes on us. Sign your names and back on your bikes."

I'm buzzing now. Chug back the water. Four minutes… we can do that. Christophe is an old man, he can't hold out. I'm not worried about Van Daele either. Whoever he is.

Time to do the maths. Four minutes, 50 km to go. If they're going at 20 km/h, then I need to up the pace during my recovery phases. Ride on the edge, that's the way to win in a race like this.

We can catch them with 10 km to go, and then I'll let the baggage go.

Henri Pélissier can do this, even with the two Belgians hanging on.

Out of Fécamp, I look round and catch Scieur dawdling. That's all it takes – a glance away from the road, a blink of the eye. A good rider is always on the lookout for that split second where his opponent is weak. Scieur is weak, and I capitalise. The gradients are tough round here, but nothing for the likes of me.

Scieur… bad rider.

A good attack comes out of nowhere, you have to be in the right gear – so that flick of the chain at the last puncture was spot on. Some of the new sprinters like to be in big gears, but I like a small gear, turns the wheels faster, and this one – with my trademark slam on the pedals – is just right. Scieur is gone, but Rossius is stronger than I thought.

Easy now, let's play with our new toy. Rossius is a Belgian, so simple of mind. You have to be clever with him because raw, brute force does not work on Belgians.

I slow up and make small talk.

"Looks like we've lost Léon. So much for the locomotive, huh?"

He shrugs. Not much of a talker for a Walloon. Let's attack again, shall we? I swing to the left, let's get him off my tail, he swings back across, so I'm swinging to the right, attack after attack, slow down, and then attack again – he's back on my wheel. Persistent little guy. I almost admire him.

So I attack again, and what does he do? He attacks me while I wait up for him. This is great. So I hit him with another Pélissier special. Cat. Mouse.

Those four minutes – surely with all these attacks, it's down to two minutes at most.

Rossius won't let go; I have to use the wind to my advantage now. Next attack will be into a headwind, it won't be easy, but it'll take him down; he's wider – big guys can't handle the wind. We're probably 20k from the finish; if it weren't for the buzz going through my body right now, the salt from the sea wind would be screaming agony into the cuts and gashes from earlier in the stage.

14 hours of racing. 14 hours. Man, this is a shit job for a superstar like me.

A small incline slows us both up, but what's this up ahead? The old man! It's him – Christophe, back-pedalling up the tiniest of bumps like he's riding his nemesis the Tourmalet. What's going on? He's hit the wall. He's hit the bloody wall.

"Finished for the day old man? Haha," I scream, I'm so delighted. This is brilliant. I'm laughing like a child.

"Fuck off stringbean," he pants back at me. Nice.

Oh this is hilarious. I'm pissing myself, it's so funny. Christophe – the old Gaul – Vercingetorix – Cri-Cri – the man with so many nicknames, they're weighing him down. And he's going backwards.

Only one more to go, and that's the unheard-of Belgian Van Daelewotsit. Oh man, this is too easy, I'll sweep him up and lose this Rossius lad – and coast into Le Havre to be welcomed as the deserving winner – the only possible winner. Ha ha! See my wheel and weep, Belgians.

Curves, into the wind, out of the wind, left of the wind, right of the wind. Why is Rossius still on my tail? Did he enjoy seeing Christophe fail?

Normandy, the land of hills and thrills. They're short and sharp; we dip in and out of seaside towns into hills and valleys, back into seaside towns, up, down, around and still the Belgian with the big legs is grunting away in my wake like a faithful dog who doesn't know his master disdains him.

Oh ho – would you look at this now? We've crested the climb and who's this in the distance? Another grey shirt, it can only be Van Daele – oh boy, I love a target. Here we go… this is a rush. On goes Rossius, which is fine – go have him. I'll save some energy for the finish in Le Havre.

We're reeling him in now, every turn of the wheel seems to bring the Belgian rider ever closer, and Rossius is working hard to pull him back. I'm waiting for that weakness, that instant of forgetfulness in Rossius, he has to break his concentration and look away… come on, Rossius, lose your focus… a shift of the eyeballs – there's my sign. I'm gone!

And I've lost him – Rossius is gone. Van Daele is behind – it's a procession! Henri Pélissier is going to win the first stage. Henri Pélissier, his first stage win of many on his way to winning the Tour de France. I've lost Rossius!

It's a long straight approach, a boring, long, flat, straight run into Le Havre, how many kilometres I don't know because the road signs are falling apart, bombed to bits some of them. I look back. He's in the distance, he can't keep up. Where are you Belgian boy? I'm a target for him, but he's flapping around. Yes! I'm going to do it, I'm going to do it. I'll be leading the Tour tonight, and there's money, money, money on offer for the first man over the line.

I'm riding into the back streets of Le Havre with Rossius in the distance, Van Daele nowhere to be seen.

Henri Pélissier, the milkman's boy come good. Oh Dad, oh brother, oh lost brother, if you could see me now. Here comes the port, here come the crowds, they're egging me on, cheering noises, a wall of sound – THIS is what the Tour is all about. THIS is what riding your bike is all about. The pain and the wounds, the mental torture, this is why you ride. Henri Pélissier, on his way to victory. Henri Péli... wait... no, not the back wheel. NO NO NO NO NO. Not now.

Not the back wheel. I'm so close. I was so close.

The chrrr, chrrr, chrrr, the sound of wooden rim on road, the sound every rider dreads, it's skidding, it's scraping, I can ride this out, yes? The tube keeps some air. I panic. Look back. Here comes Rossius – I'm going to have to get out of the saddle and hit the pedals harder than ever. Forget the puncture, just ride, just ride.

No please, God, no, don't do this to me. Don't take my wheel now.

A gust of wind, is that the breeze or is it Rossius? It's

him, I can see him, pounding his pedals, dancing into the distance as my machine lets me down, and without any celebration, without any respect for the man he's beaten, without even the slightest hint of joy, he rides over the line to take the win, and I'm doing all I can to push this beaten, broken bike to the finish. I'm hammering down with each pedal stroke; I'm going nowhere.

There's an old man at the side of the road, his raincoat drenched and his hair flapping in the wind.

"No luck, son," he seems to be saying.

Second place.

Rossius has gone into the café to sign on already, crowds around him slapping him on the back. They'll take a Belgian as their own. Not one of them would have known. This stage was mine. Stupid fucking bike. Stupid tyre.

Around me, no one. Just the old man with the wet raincoat.

No luck, son.

Stage 1

1	Jean Rossius (BEL)	15h 56' 00"
2	Henri Pélissier (FRA)	+ 1' 15"
3	Joseph Van Daele (BEL)	+ 2' 10"
4	Eugène Christophe (FRA)	+ 5' 41"
5	Léon Scieur (BEL)	+ 9' 22"
6	Alfred Steux (BEL)	+ 10' 47"
7	Lucien Buysse (BEL)	+ 26' 27"
8	Hector Tiberghien (BEL)	+ 26' 53"
9	Émile Masson (BEL)	+ 27' 53"
10	Firmin Lambot (BEL)	+ 29' 59"

STAGE 2
LE HAVRE TO CHERBOURG

Eugene Christophe

Does Alavoine never sleep? I look at my watch and sigh. 3am.

"And so – ha – I thought to myself: what's the point? Why push yourself?"

I grunt. He carries on.

"And there I was, side of the road, gasping for breath, and I looked at the ditch and said – you know what – I'm going to have a kip."

Silence, it seems, won't stop him.

"So I said to the driver – ha – you'll have to wake me up in twenty, twenty should do it, yes? He said you're a fool Jean-lad, a total fool, and I said – ha – we'll see who's the fool at the end of the day – ha!"

I turn over, my back to him. Still he goes on.

"I mean, old Desgrange, who does he think he is – sending us out on a 5,500km race when we're all out of shape? Eh? Who does he think he is?"

"I know." Now leave me alone.

"I mean, look at me!" He pats his belly, I can hear the empty thump of open palm on stomach. "I'm a whopper."

"Mm-hm."

"So if a man can't have a nap after 200km of racing, what can he do? Hm? Eh Cri-Cri? Hm? Eh?"

"Mm."

Annoying as he is, he's right. He is a bit chubby, and this race is ridiculous. Desgrange should have known the roads were unsuitable. I saw one boy crying by the side of the road, crying his eyes out, his back wheel buckled. A few of the boys in the café afterwards were telling Desgrange where he could put his race, and I'll tell you – it wasn't something you'd want your mother to hear.

"What is it that makes us ride a race like this, hey? Hm? Cri-Cri?"

I feign sleep.

But I think I know the answer. It's this or the workshop. And I reckon we're a bit different to most men. There has to be something different about you if you actually want to race 14 to 16 hours every other day. There's something twisted about you if you raced Paris-Roubaix or the Tour of the Battlefields – and you came back for more. You thought to yourself – hey, that was hell, I'll do that again.

I think Alavoine has finally gone off to sleep. Or he believes I'm asleep.

I lie stock still – any movement could indicate I'm faking it. These sheets are louder than the rain outside. Desgrange believes punishment should be round-the-clock.

Maybe Alavoine's right – what's the point?

Machurey

So I had a telegram from Henri, I did. A short one, they always are short, and it said:

40 riders left Honfleur stop Prepare food stop

Well that was at 9 o'clock and if the Auto's right then they should be through here by, what, 11 at the latest? But these roads, this weather, I can't see anyone being here by 11, not even the German army.

It was easier before the war, as was everything I suppose, but getting a whole feeding station ready for 40 riders when nobody's got any food anywhere… Henri's got ideas above his station, he has.

Old Madame Bosquet was up all night with me making the bread. She used to run the local boulangerie, had no time for us men any more, she said. Us and our fighting. I said Madame, we were defending ourselves, defending our honour, defending you - no I stopped short of that - she was having none of it, said we'd been squaring up for a fight since the Prussians came in 1871, well that was that, I said she could make the bread, I'll make the chops and we'll keep it at that; no more conversation, no more talk unless she wanted to talk about bike racing which is what everyone wants to talk about these days, thanks to us. But she's not into bike racing either.

She fumed in her corner of the kitchen and I fumed in mine.

It's good to get back to the routine. Every tour, it goes like this: I go ahead to the day's main feeding station and get fed by the local dignitaries who are just overjoyed at having the tour come through their town, then I procure the food from the local farmers, boulangers, butchers, use a local restaurant, enjoy some local wine (if in the south) or local firewater (if in the north) and spend the night with the team getting the day's food ready.

Best month of the year, this. Or at least, it usually is, but this year we're scrabbling around for whatever we can get. Pork chops, now there's plenty of them, the Germans kept the pigs alive - they even looked after them. Telling who you care for in hard times, isn't it. Rice cakes, we've got cars full of them, but you have riders who stuff their gobs good and proper, riders like Lambot who turn up at the start line with ten baguettes full of ham, cheese, butter, jam, and wotnot, and that's just for starters, he's had the lot before he's out of the neutralised part of the race, and then you have others like that young lad who turned up with his parents, well you just want to do well by them don't you.

Now we're "trying to get back to normal", I'm stuck here with old Madame Bosquet, whose son has skulked off somewhere, probably to avoid his mother no doubt, trying to make the best out of a bad lot.

So Henri's telegram came, and I ran outside where the crowds were already braving the rain - funny lot these Normans - and I shouted "They've left Honfleur" which got everyone a-talking, it did, word went round the town as quick as wildfire, except if it were wildfire it would have been put out by the rain. Like I say, funny lot. You could hear them all calculating and debating - "oh so if they've left Honfleur and they're going at 22km/h then they'll be here in… oh no, you've got it all wrong, they're going at 25km/h at least… oh no you're not thinking about the headwind, it's a headwind all the way... no, no, tailwind..." And so on.

And they've really come out for the Tour, they have. Old Henri, he knows how to put on a show. The first ones came around 6 in the morning, a little ambitious, but they got to the checkpoint and that's what matters most in the Tour - if you can get to the checkpoint positions first, a rider might ask you to hold his bike while he stuffs his pockets with baguettes and chops and omelettes and rice cakes. They'll get to see them stuffing their faces and pockets at the same time, keeping an eye on each other for which rider does a runner first. Entertainment at its finest.

So if you're a proper fan then you want to be here, by the feeding station, where you can get right up close to your heroes.

And if you're a proper fan then you know that watching the Tour de France is a day's work for five minutes' reward, except that your day's work involves standing around with no hope of a chair or relief for hours on end, before the peloton flashes by, and it's usually them flashing by in different colours at least so you know who's who - oh aye, there's Petit Breton, God rest his soul, in his light blue and white, or Christophe, the old Gaul, in the red and blue hoops, but now they're all in grey, it could be Adam and Eve for all you know. Or Adam and Steve.

Every telegram I get, I duly shout it out. These poor souls soaked to their skin latch on to every word - 11:30, Deauville - so they say - and everyone's chattering doing their calculations "they must be through here by half twelve at worst… we'll be home by lunchtime…"

And yet, still nothing. You look down the road, hoping for a car, some kind of indication that the Tour is on its way, and the rain just pours, the wind just blows, and the empty road stays empty.

And now a conundrum - a right proper conundrum, this one. You want to do right by the riders, you do, you want them to arrive at the station and you've got the chops all warm and the chicken legs nice and crispy, and you've heard they've left Deauville so you're doing the calculations yourself, and you're thinking - well, do I warm them up now or will they be late again? I worked it out, they were an hour late into Honfleur, and they were probably an hour late into Caen as well, so what might happen between Caen and Arromanches?

Oh Henri, send us a message. Something.

That's it - they're going in the oven. I call over Rouze and Sallient, my local dedicated help - "Get the ovens on - these will need fifteen minutes." They run over, all in a flap. Marhaut is over, too - sweeping up the chops and the bread.

"No, leave the bread, that's fine - there'll be no room. Just get the meats in the ovens as quickly as you can. Don't overdo it."

I've got an armful of chicken legs and I'm carrying about twenty omelettes on a platter. A delicate old balancing act. I bet Mme Bosquet is pissing herself from that window up there - look at him, old fancy pants with his bike racing, look at him balancing those omelettes in the rain. I curse her silently. Marhaut has chops all down his front, but at least he's holding up. Rouze - the younger of my helpers - is doing a fine job opening the doors in time as we prance over the cobbles to the kitchens. And then a clatter from behind us - Sallient is down.

"Chuffing hell, Sallient, why are you carrying the pans? We don't need pans, we're putting the food in the ovens."

"But I thought…"

"You thought what? We'd put the pans in the oven? I'll put a pan round your head in a minute. Put them back where they were."

And then… of all things… a car! Like an angel from heaven, descending from the clouds - your torment will soon be over Machurey, your deed is done. They'll be here soon. And once they're gone, you'll have a chop to yourself, feet up, glass of Calvados, perhaps. Ah, the Tour.

It's Desmarets. Never have I been so pleased to see his ugly face.

"Oi Machurey," he swings his wretched mug out of the open car window, quickly realising it's raining and retracting it immediately. So I guess that means I have to approach the car. Typical.

"What's the news? Are they on their way?"

He snarls back "of course they're on their way, Machurey, what do you think they're doing? Sipping martinis on the beach?"

What a lovely man.

He leans out and surveys the feeding station. Disapprovingly, that is.

"Where's the fucking food Mach? You've got 20 minutes – we've got 10 riders on their way. Sort it. Now!"

20 minutes? Oh the relief. 20 minutes! I could dance on air, I could - 20 minutes? That'll be plenty of time to get the temperature down to a manageable level - 20 minutes, I shout, and I hear Rouze cheering from the kitchens. I hear Mme Bosquet's spit hit the bucket up on the third floor. I hear the murmur go through the crowd and the noise levels rise. I hear them cheering Desmarets as he drives off, sounding his horn like the leader of a triumphant army. Fool.

Those 20 minutes flash by - and the noise builds to a crescendo outside. The boys get everything ready and another car is on the way - Desgrange this time, oh boy do they love him. You'd have thought it was Clemenceau on the back of a camel by the noise they were making. It's hard to make out what he's saying but we're down to 9 riders, in five minutes. I think.

And then they're on us in a flash - the crowd have broken free of the barriers and they're surrounding the Pélissiers, or at least you think it's the Pélissiers, everyone is grey, and everyone is covered in mud, but Henri P, you know him straight away. Rossius is there, you know him from the size of his legs - like Bayonne ham - they're tearing away at the table, they are, taking whatever they can, stuffing their bags and their pockets with food. Rouze is pulling food back from this big Belgian lad, Heusghem or something his name is, he's trying to take more than his single bag's worth and I think a fight's going to break out.

Eugène Christophe is there, sorting everything out as usual - there's a bit of confusion when Masson pulls in to town and he's looking for someone to hold his bike while he gets some food - oi, Masson, take your food, and he's rushing like a goose, but no one will hold it for him and finally a pregnant woman steps forward - she's got at least three in there, you'd think - and he's holding his bike trying to be a gentleman and she's trying to rip it from him saying "let me hold your bike, I'm hardly going to nick off with it", and the other riders are pissing themselves laughing. Alavoine pulls up and gives her a kiss, holds the bike himself for a while, and then they're all gone.

I survey the damage. There's food on the floor, broken rice cakes and chicken bones - but there's still bags to be taken. A little respite from the frenzy, before another group comes in - this young lad Mottiat, how much does he need? Marhaut is trying to hold back the chops but Mottiat's stronger than him - says something about him being the entertainment. They both are today.

The stragglers pull in. Léon Scieur is all mud and blood, a riding wounded, says he fell outside Arromanches on the col into town, he spends ten minutes carrying out repairs before he gets to the food, and then in come the Buysse brothers, crying their eyes out - get us home, we give up, we've had enough - can't do it any more, leave us alone, get off us. They're pushing at the crowd, who are pushing them back on their bikes. No one is quitting this race – the two Belgians are literally pushed out of town by twenty men in cloth caps. Race, boys. Race. I think Marcel was still crying into his handlebars as he tried to evade the hands of the French fans who've been here since 6, standing in the rain, waiting for a moment like this, a moment they can take home back to the factory or the bar or the workshop, a moment they can savour. And with that, there are no more riders - just fans tearing apart the last of the chicken legs and trying to get their hands on the omelettes the riders didn't want.

We take cover underneath the awning.

"You leaving yet?" shouts Mme Bosquet out of her window.

"See you next year, you deaf old bag."

"I heard that!"

Léon Scieur

"Are you sure I can't help you?"

The old woman's almost pleading. She can see I'm shivering. The thread won't come loose, no matter how hard I try.

"They'll throw me out of the race," I say, which is true. The commissioner - rain-sodden and miserable - nods in agreement. He's been standing there ever since I punctured, cap held low over his head, raincoat dripping huge globulets onto the ground. The grim reaper would be better company, I swear.

"No help. Not even someone to hold the needle."

"Then this man is a bastard," she offers. I smile, because

yes. Yes, he is. And it's refreshing to hear an old lady curse.

I've been sitting on this woman's doorstep for the last ten minutes, sheltering from the rain and the wind, trying to repair my latest puncture, the latest of how many, I've lost count. Seven? Eight? So many I now have to rip out the inner tube, repair it, and hope I get to the finish line on this alone.

She's kind enough to offer some light, which is welcome in these grey lands. For a July afternoon, this is the darkest I've known it.

"I tell you what you can do, madam, bring that lamp a little closer, it'll warm my hands."

And it does, a small circle of warmth is enough to revive my fingers, momentarily. I grab some thread and pull. It's coming. I ran out of inner tubes this morning, somewhere near Caen. I stopped in a bike shop on the outskirts of town, but they'd sold their last set, probably to some upstart like Pélissier, or Pélissier's butler. So now I'm repairing the last inner tube itself, unstitch it, bind it, restitch it. This takes time, and concentration.

"What is your story, young man?" This old lady is a dear.

"You mean my war story?" She nods. All stories are war stories.

"Well, I'm Belgian. I got caught on the wrong side of the lines."

They probably don't get many Belgians in Isigny-sur-Mer. There's a look of confusion on her face. We all have our war stories, we all lived them so intensely.

I wonder what hers is.

"I mean to say, when the Germans invaded I couldn't escape. At first, every day you woke up and you asked yourself - will this be my last day? Will someone save us? And then... you realise every morning you're still alive, so you get used to it."

That surprises her. "How can you get used to occupation? These Boches, they're animals."

"Oh they are the worst, Madam, you're right. I used to ride with Marcel Kerff, you've probably never heard of him, but he was a good man, a fine boy. When he heard the Germans were in the forest, he wanted to see what was happening, that's all - just wanted to go see what all the fuss was about. We knew they were bad, but Marcel - he didn't know how bad they could be. Innocent as the day was young, was Kerff, and he'd have won this here race one day, I swear. He'd have been a true champion. And what did they do to him? Hanged him for being a spy."

The tube is coming loose, at last. I search for the hole with my forefinger. An expert, me.

Poor Marcel. The peloton is poorer for the lack of him. There are gaps everywhere. A gap for Octave, a gap for Lucien, a gap for François, but a gap a mile wide for a man like Marcel.

"Marcel wasn't alone," I carry on, "whole towns came out to the border that week to see the German artillery. Back in those days, it was something you'd marvel at, before it steamrollered you. Look at these men - look at their machines - we were just factory boys on our bikes, no more than that, and this technology - this manpower rolls into the forest nearby. What do you do? You go look. We just never thought they'd stay so long."

"The poor boy. But you, what did you do to stay alive?"

She asks good questions, this Madame.

"I kept a low profile. I guessed that if they picked out Marcel, they'd pick out other cyclists. We're mobile, we're fast – if you were recruiting a spy, you'd hire a cyclist. If you think about it, we were sort-of famous, and we all guessed that we'd be a scalp for the Boche. But then, the longer you stay alive, the more daring you got."

"How so?" She leans in. I've lost so much time on this stage, I might as well finish my story.

"I had a garage - car repairs, mostly. Bike repairs too," I nod down at the nearly-finished inner tube, my eighth in two days' racing, and one that needs to get me to Dieppe non-stop. She smiles. "We had a nice trade in excursions on the side, people wanted to see the damage… until the Boche found out and confiscated the vehicles, but that kept us going for a couple of years. I guess it's the same everywhere, we were all looking for moments of light relief among the darkness. You know."

She knows.

The stitching is almost complete now. I've become something of a pro. I look out at the rain, and the commissioner - smoking underneath the lady's coal shed, a black outline with an orange dot - has given up on me. Like I've given up on the race.

"And here, Madam? How was your war?"

A look. I know that look, I've seen it a thousand times since the Armistice.

"Quiet. It was so quiet. Everyone left, and we fell silent that day. You stopped talking and started reading peoples' faces – is he still alive? Is he perished? And then we waited for people to come back. And we waited, and we never forgot, and most of us are still waiting."

"You lost men?"

"We all did. My husband died before the war, but our sons never came home, God rest their souls."

"I'm sorry to hear that." I've stopped fixing my wheel. There are too many stories like this. We listen to the silence, in between raindrops.

She fixes herself. "Listen to me, I'm sure you've got a race to ride, and your wheel looks all but fixed now. You're a good man… sorry, I never even asked your name."

"Léon, Madame."

"Léon. Good name. A solid name. Where are you from, Léon? Which town?"

"Florennes, Madame. Florennes."

Henri Pélissier

B rother, dear brother. You came so close.

Ah yes, you see – today is Henri Pélissier's day – although dear brother, I'd have let you win, really I would. But old Henri Desgrange, he'd have had my guts for garters if I'd shown any weakness for you.

And so it was, the faster of the two remaining brothers prevailed at the line. Mother nature gave me the legs, dear brother. Maybe in Brittany, you'll have the better of me.

Still, you pushed me all the way, as you always did.

Remember, Francis, the day I got my first bike? You were four, but boy you wanted to ride it and then you cried all night Dad said you kept the cows awake.

Remember when I came home from my sickness at granny's in Polminhac with my second bike? The better bike, the one with the quick tyres. You took my old bike, rode around with milk jugs on the handlebars, never spilled a drop you said, but you just made me go faster.

Ah, you see – that's the motivation. No older brother wants to get beaten by little brother. Could you imagine the humiliation, Francis?

Ah Francis. Number 2. And so shall you remain. Remember how we'd race through the Yvelines together? How you cried every time I beat you back to the farm? And yet here you are, chasing me to the finishing line.

Oh I admit that I did regret leaving you that day when I met Lucien. The Petit-Breton said I was a talent, and he'd know. Lucien took me under his wing, saw in me a younger version of himself, I guess – a father who wanted his son to submit to a life of peasantry and drudgery, a father who hated the bicycle. Lucien and I, we flew that day. We flew away from you, from the flat lands and the milking cows, we flew from the mediocrity and the humdrum of the farms and the factories. He taught me to settle for nothing other than the best.

Of course, you followed eventually. You always did. Like you're following me into the Café de Paris right now. And brother, you are a bother, but I love you like no other.

Hear that noise, dear brother? Oh yes, it's for me. No – I must show some humility – it's for us. The two Pélissiers, thoroughbred racers that we are, triumphant against a peloton of grim, grey-shirted no-hopers. Strike up the orchestra, boys, the talent is here.

Ah, the public love a Pélissier. Me first, Francis.

Smile, boys, smile despite the hurt. Put on a show for Henri Desgrange and his travelling slavery show. Yes, yes, I know, we look so fresh, we look so fresh.

Look at Desgrange, his moustache twirled to perfection, his pen poised, his stories probably already written despite what we have to say. We look so fresh.

I'll give you Fresh, Henri, Fresh is 15 hours in the saddle, riding into wind and rain, splattered in mud and shit. I'm surprised I could detach myself from the saddle. Hardly anyone can tell the difference between us (I'm the good looking one, obviously), so disfigured are we by mud and blood. This is Fresh. I'm creased all over, my back is screaming in agony and now I'm being squeezed by a walrus-man with a prickly beard and Francis, you're in the clutches of a woman, is it a woman? You can hardly tell these days.

Oh, the noise, though, the noise… where do we sign?

And here he is, the ringmaster Desgrange and his cronies, beaming from ear to ear. "Which Pélissier is this?" he booms, making sure to stay well away from this walking mud-mountain, soaking in the second-hand adulation. "You can barely tell the difference between them, eh, Alphonse!"

Baugé doesn't give a shit, we're not riding for him.

"Where do I sign, Papa Desgrange?"

"Right here, lad – are you staying for a drink? Welcome home the other riders?"

"What do you think?" It's a rhetorical question. Of course we're not staying for a drink. They serve vin de pays with some second-rate charcuterie, and the last thing we need is to see their miserable faces as they traipse in, all bitter and twisted.

"Besides," I can't resist, "watching these workhorses slouch through the door at the end of a hard day's work is depressing. Thoroughbreds don't hang around to watch the donkeys come home, Henri."

We've got a hotel room to get to. A first, searing, stinging bath and then another bath, as many baths as it takes to wash away the pain and the scars and the shit from our bodies, and if we're lucky, and there's any skin left, we'll have another bath in the morning while we hide away from you, Desgrange, as you knock on our doors for your second-rate interviews about what we do on our day off.

Francis, dear brother, follow me.

As you always do.

Stage 2

1	Henri Pélissier (FRA)	15h 51' 13"
2	Francis Pélissier (FRA)	+ 1"
3	Honoré Barthélémy (FRA)	+ 3' 47"
4	Jean Alavoine (FRA)	s.t.
5	Jean Rossius (BEL)	+ 4' 40"
6	Émile Masson (BEL)	+ 9' 04"
7	Eugène Christophe (FRA)	+ 15' 25"
8	Firmin Lambot (BEL)	+ 17' 37"
9	Félix Goethals (FRA)	+ 56' 03"
10	Urbain Anseeuw (fr) (BEL)	s.t.

General Classification

1	Henri Pélissier (FRA)	
2	Eugène Christophe (FRA)	+ 19' 52"
3	Jean Rossius (BEL)	+ 33' 25"

STAGE 3
CHERBOURG TO BREST

Honoré Barthélémy

Ah man. I should be in bed. This is proper wrong.

Me first Tour, and me nuggets – that's me toes to you – are all over the shop. Especially the right big nugget, which is ingrowing and it looks a right proper mess. And it stinks. If it stinks right now, at the start of a stage, you can imagine what it's going to smell like when we're in Brittany tonight.

I'll wrap it in a crepe and soak it in cider. That's probably what the locals do over there.

And I know Mr Baugé is meant to be lookin' after us and all that, but nobody washed me jersey so that's stinking too, I smell like cheese today.

Ah man. This is shit. I didn't even sleep last night, or this afternoon which is what Mr Christophe said I should be doing, I was too excited, man, I was pumped up. Heart was all a-flutter, I was like muscles twitching and my mind was going all over the place, I couldn't sleep in the afternoon, but Mr Christophe, he's been doing this since I was a nipper, back when everyone had them big moustaches, and he was like "Noré, lad, you need to sleep if you're going to race in the morning, get some rest," and he even said he'd look at me gearing, but I got all embarrassed, like, y'know, a big man like Mr Christophe having a look at me bike, and I bet the pedals stink of foot cheese.

Naw, you're alright, I told him, and he said any time I needed a hand.

He's a good man. I like Mr Christophe.

I really stink, man. Really stink. I might be imagining it, but there's a bit more personal space than usual.

So I'm just mooching around at the start, and trying to stay warm because here in Cherbourg, it's real nippy and the rain it hasn't actually stopped once. This fella comes up to me, and I know he's one of Mr Baugé's men because he's always at the dinner table stuffing his face every night, like a prisoner who's having his first meal after being let out, y'know, really hungry all the time and he puts his face really low down to the bowl like if it drops, it won't splash out and he won't lose any. That's how hungry he is.

He's wearing a trenchcoat, and he's saying something funny, and I'm saying what? Wossat? Speaky the Frenchy?

"You want socks?"

I'm well miffed, man. I mean, have a heart, I haven't even started racing yet, I know they smell mate, but have a heart.

"Are you having a laugh, fella?" I'm serious an' all. I put on my proper serious face.

"No, mate, serious – you want socks? I've got loads of them. Look."

And he has. And I remember who he is now and why I can't understand him. Goethals his name is, from up north somewhere, Calais or Boulogne probably, he looks like he really should be selling socks now I come to think about it. Got one of them little moustaches that makes him look Italian, but in a cheap way, y'know, like a cheap Italian who sells socks but he's almost Belgian. Even his flat cap makes him look more dodgy than he probably is.

Man, this Tour, it's full of all sorts. Italian-Belgian men with tiny moustaches selling socks before a stage.

He's opening up his trenchcoat and showing me all kinds of socks, some good socks too, some nice designs on them, even in the dark you can appreciate the styles although I like the plain ones as you can mix and match them and nobody notices if you haven't paired them, and I'm like, man, I could do with some new socks but you're going to have to wait until tonight, I need some bonuses from Papa Henri so I can pay for them. He's like, yeah, OK, if you make it, maybe see you in Brittany, and you get the idea he's not going to make it tonight. Quicker just to go home.

And with that, off he skulks, opening up his trenchcoat to other riders, so maybe it's not me nuggets that's the problem.

Ah man. Can't we just go? I hate hanging around at the start. It's freezing and it's dark and there's a hint of rain coming, and the smell from that Belgian's pipe is getting on me wick. Coomans it is, one of the Belgians, puffing away, makes me cough. How do you race like that?

I shuffle along a few riders to get away from the pipe smell, reminds me of me Dad. Funny how everyone here's reminded of their Dad all the time. Me Dad hated the bike, me Dad didn't want me riding a bike, me Dad this, me Dad that. Dads didn't like bikes because they were dangerous and they couldn't keep up with you. Get on with it. Ride on.

Mr Christophe is on his own. Should I go speak to him?

Yes. No. Yes.

No.

Oh, he's noticed me. He's got a twinkle in his eye. Tousled hair and a proper friendly look about him. Coming this way. I stand up straight.

"Young Barthélémy, let's see your gearing."

He's eyeing up my back wheel. Ah man, have I got the right gearing or not? I'm feeling the pressure here, proper feeling it.

"You'll do well to stay all day in that gear, lad. You planning to flip it at any point?"

I wasn't planning on flipping at all, actually. But this is Mr Christophe, Mr Tour de France – play it cool.

"Yeah, Mr Christophe, I thought I'd flip after breakfast."

"Ah, good lad," he looks happy with that. Full marks Noré! Slap on the back for me.

"Tell you what, catch up with me after breakfast, we'll go for a spin, yes?"

"Yes sir", I blub. Mr Christophe wants to go for a spin with me. I don't know what that means, but I guess it's good, yes? Go for a spin? Is that pre-war speak?

I hear someone shouting, it must be time to go. Mr Christophe is on his bike, he has this little routine, everything about Mr Christophe is routine. Maybe I should learn a thing or two from him; look how he bounces up and down on his saddle a couple of times. Puts his foot into his stirrups, these things that he invented, I got them too, Mr Baugé said that Mr Christophe is a great inventor and you can see him now, the great inventor, rubbing his arms, smacking his cheeks, hunching down on his handlebars. The great man, the old Gaul.

I should develop my own routine. I'll have to think about that one.

Oh aye, and we're gone, rooooaaaaarrrrrr goes the crowd

like a massive lion, and the rooossshhhhhh they're going all quiet because we're moving and they're not, but you can still sort of hear them if you really try, you can hear the band in the café, if you try. And then you can't, all you can hear is the engines of the cars and the rattling of wheels and the thud of potholes and stones against rims. You hear the early morning sound of men struggling to stay focused, grunts and yawns, farts and stretches, and the screeching of brakes at turns you can't see, and man, the smell of the car and guess who… Goethals is riding next to me.

"I've got some socks in the support car" he says, or at least I think that's what he's saying cos it sounds like "I'sh got shome shocks in the shupport car". That Goethals, man, he's well dodgy.

I need to find Mr Christophe. Go for a spin.

Eugène Christophe

This Tour has been… cold. This morning is little better. A coastal wind is whipping in at us, and a little solidarity from the organisers wouldn't have gone amiss. Bob Desmarets, for one. I see him, half asleep in his blanket, half awake with a mouth full of crepe. Warm, sated, ready to doze off.

Don't think I can't see you, Bob. Don't worry about me, I'll write your headlines for you.

Solidarity, that's all we ask. Suffer for your art, Bob.

Jean-lad keeps them coming. "Oi, Fat Bob, you forgot a crepe – it's there under your third chin!"

Roars of laughter. I love Jean-lad, although not when I have to share a hotel room with him. Kept me up all night

53

after the first stage with his tales of sleeping in a ditch. I told him he's an idiot – 20 minutes could be worth a lot to a sprinter like him. A sprinter who can climb, too. That could be the difference between winning and losing the Tour.

"Hey, Desgrange, keep your eyes on the road, if they're still working!"

Come dawn, we've had enough of each other. Desgrange hangs back, and the peloton pulls apart a little. Familiarity breeds contempt, and thankfully in the middle of summer, sun comes up earlier in the day, so each man discovers his true personality once more. Jean-lad will spend most of the day sharing anecdotes or cheating, while the young lad Barthélémy spends most of the time at the back moaning about his ingrowing toenail, or worse, moaning about the coverage his ingrowing toenail is getting in the paper.

Henri Pélissier is usually looking for a wheel to suck, so long as it's useful, while Firmin Lambot is carefully studying each rider for signs of weakness, hoping to tick them off on his long list of riders to eliminate. Note to all – Lambot especially – we are increasingly few. In Paris, there were 68 of us, now I count barely 30, so in two days of racing, we've lost more than half the field. Firmin might win this thing after all, on his own.

I look around and the peloton is barely awake. A few yawns from Mottiat and Coomans, Alavoine is hanging off the back, not looking himself.

So I attack. And I attack hard. I'm using a 47 x 17/18 gearing ratio today, which is perfect for the flatter parts of the stage. I've got a 19/20 on the other side of the wheel – so if I really need something extra, I can stop, flip my back wheel around, and use one of those gears. Old man Desgrange doesn't like us changing gears, stopped us from using derailleurs, but at least we're not on fixed gear bikes!

The key to a good attack is to spin your wheels as fast as you can on the lowest gear you've got, so have your wheel ready for that. Sprinters like Alavoine, they use the smallest cog possible, but I'm not a sprinter – more a rouleur – so I tend to go up a cog or two and use some power in the thighs to pound away at the pedals. There are some new riders who claim that you require a bigger gear in a sprint, but there's no substitute for being able to power your legs more quickly.

To my delight, nobody has gone with me. Dawn, alone, somewhere outside of Coutances, and the red sky augurs well. I'll target the sun today, if it shows its face.

I look around, there's a few shouts and arguments in the peloton, or what's left of the peloton, it seems to have split and they're arguing over who's going to chase me. Oh come on, gents, give me some time on my own. That's my encouragement to push on again, I'm giving the pedals a proper lashing. Let's have another look round.

Still arguing.

Jean Alavoine

There's two pelotons right now, and I'm in neither of them. What would I call myself? The third, and smallest peloton? The broom peloton? A unique band of one?

Last place Alavoine. Alavoine All Alone. That's quite funny, I might keep that.

Oh-ho, who's this? It looks like Rossius has had his chips, just as the rain starts to come down (again), the little Belgian is sat by the side of the road with his wheel hanging off, and he's blubbing like a little child. Ha! Bet you any money Eugène will be moaning about your modern riders not knowing how to repair bikes... I can hear him now. "In my day, we'd be walking ten hours to the local blacksmith we would, repair it all by yourself, even if it takes two days, you'd get back on your bike and you'd finish the stage all on your own, never leave a job half done."

Ha, I do amuse myself.

What's wrong with me today? I'm dawdling like a cyclo-tourist. In fact, I'm dawdling with a cyclo-tourist.

"Hello, young chap."

"Are you Jean Alavoine?" he asks.

"I might be, I might not be. What's the difference?"

"Can I ride with you for a bit?"

"Come on then sunshine – see if you can hold my wheel."

Aha, that was just the tonic I needed. The embarrassment of a cyclo-tourist trying to hang onto my wheel is enough, and I see the peloton up ahead, not too far that I can't catch them. Your man is trying gamely to hang on.

I think of poor Rossius as I reel in the peloton. You know, not everyone can handle a forge or build themselves a new saddle with sticks and leaves or something. That poor guy probably delivers letters in Belgium for a living, and he's had a shit Tour so far. That 30-minute penalty for giving Thys a drink was a joke, a proper joke, especially as Thys went home the next day in a huff, and Rossius won the stage. Now he's probably walking to the next checkpoint with his bike over his shoulder. First train back to Belgium.

A few cheery faces as I rejoin the peloton and make my way through.

Ahoy-hoy, let the boy through. Henri Pélissier, you old dog, I thought you'd be long gone. Old man Christophe, I've got a story for you, you know that Belgian guy with the ham hocks for legs – well he's only gone and broken his bike.

"Fixing it, then, is he?"

Here we go.

Henri Pélissier

Attack me on a puncture, will you? Dogs! Scumbags!

I'll show you how a roadman rides. Who was it who went? Christophe – typical. Lambot – who cares. Alavoine – well, he has some weight to lose. Goethals, Chassot – I can mop them up in no time.

I ride on anger today. Every rider has his own fuel, mine is fury. Those opportunists, those dogs. I'll show them.

Henri Desgrange

Did I happen to mention that this Tour has been rather a success thus far? Bob, dear boy, we're here, Brest, snap out of your reverie, and look at this place.

There are men on the rooftops, men in the trees, women in every window, and they're cheering the Brasier as it ambulates gently through the town. Ah Brest, you never let us down. First things first, I must go congratulate some of the local dignitaries for putting on such a show.

"Monsieur Devoyon, congratulations on such an orderly stage finish," – please do remember, dearest reader, that congratulating the police officer in charge is the absolute first thing you must do, he is the first person you must approach even in the presence of royalty. It gives him a sense of enormous importance, fills him with pride, and ensures that he completes the job he's set out to do. Or paid to do. Now, where's the mayor?

Nowhere to be seen, but I'll tell you who can be seen and that's the American army who are putting on a real show. Of course, the Americans are everywhere, you know them by the khaki, oh and they're playing the Marseillaise, how quite wonderful. Now, say what you like about the Americans, they came to our rescue whether we wanted them to or not, but most importantly, they've showed our men what valour truly is. In my opinion, they can stay as long as they like, or at least until we've learned this valuable lesson. There'll be no more Germans crossing our borders so long as we've got these boys around.

Ah there's Mayor Masson.

"Dear boy, what a show, what a show, you must be so proud."

He says something incomprehensibly Breton, and I'm reminded that this language really must be stamped out, obliterated, wiped from the records, like all regional languages but it's a particularly sticky one, old Breton. Onwards, Henri, onwards, the riders will be here in 10 minutes, and you have to break the bad news to them, steel yourself Henri.

What's that? The bad news? Ah yes, so here's the story. I contacted Masson and his adjoint, Hervagaud and tried to negotiate hotel rooms for the riders, which normally isn't a problem but in Brest, it seems, every hotel room in the city is taken up by army officials or Bretons from around the region who have decided to stick around the extra couple of nights to see our boys off as they head south. And indeed, I have been attempting to procure rooms for the riders for many months, rooms with baths, at the very least, but alas...

So, for the boys from la Sportive, no hotel. Rather inconvenient.

I do believe the Pélissiers have sorted themselves out, as they always do, considering they're not part of La Sportive. They're very much riding on their own ticket, but for Bauge's boys I'm afraid it's the barracks, an unwelcome reminder of the last five years, but a bed nonetheless.

I have utterly no idea what the B-licence riders are doing, but frankly, I haven't a care. I'm sure they'll look after themselves.

So, to the Café du Commerce, and an inspection of the checkpoint, if I could get in to the café, that is. Trouble with running a hugely successful Tour de France is that every man and his dog wants to clap their eyes on your riders.

Riders that are, it appears, on the way. There's a roar that starts down the boulevard, the Brestois are hanging from the poplars that line the boulevard, so they've got an advance warning that the competitors are on their way, and that noise starts to flow all the way up the boulevard. As do the rumours. Alavoine, someone says. No, it's Christophe. They're Belgian, says another. How can they tell? Everyone's in grey. The speculation of the masses.

I rush to take my place with Masson and his adjoint, and the first two are bombing down the boulevard. Could it be the Pélissiers again? 1 and 2? Or 2 and 1? Who can tell? But what a duel. One is chasing the other – he's catching him – but the lead Pélissier is dancing on his wheels, he's slightly shorter so it must be the younger boy, Francis. Henri is the skinny one, I turn to Masson and tell him these are our finest boys, the Pélissiers, our very finest.

Breton again. Tsk.

Henri can't keep up the pace, are we seeing Francis win a stage? We are! Oh Francis, my dear boy, Francis, you've only gone and done it. And how do you know for sure it's Francis and not Henri who has won? Because he looks genuinely surprised! It's a wonderful thing to see, a young man with such raw potential, a future giant of the road – no, a current giant of the road, defeating his brother with a burst of absolute raw power and tenacity. Well done, boy, well done.

Sorry, Masson, got to go, must dash, things to do, paperwork to sort out, will see you shortly, and we'll have that dinner, yes?

Not if you respond in Breton again, boy.

I push through the crowds, rough suits and hairy men, the smell of sweat and smoke, cheap cologne, get out of my way, people, get out of my way.

"Francis!" I yell, and proffer my hand. "Dear boy, you only went and did it!"

But the Pélissier boy is in no mood to celebrate, it seems. He growls at me, tells me to "fuck right off" or some vernacular that no doubt they picked up on the farm. The boy's covered in mud, and it's only then I realise that I was talking to Henri, the plucky loser. Not a good loser, mind you. Not a good one at all.

There's Francis, slightly smaller and rounder, and beaming all over.

"Francis, dear boy!"

"Monsieur Desgrange," he yells, "I bloody won a stage! How much have I won?"

"Dear boy, one thing at a time…"

Money, money – some riders only think of the money.

Stage 3

1	Francis Pélissier (FRA)	15h 30' 05"
2	Henri Pélissier (FRA)	s.t.
3	Jean Alavoine (FRA)	+ 3' 19"
4	Félix Goethals (FRA)	s.t.
5	Jules Masselis (BEL)	s.t.
6	Émile Masson (BEL)	s.t.
7	Eugène Christophe (FRA)	s.t.
8	Alfred Steux (BEL)	s.t.
9	Louis Mottiat (BEL)	s.t.
10	Honoré Barthélémy (FRA)	s.t

General Classification

1	Henri Pélissier (FRA)	
2	Eugène Christophe (FRA)	+ 23' 10"
3	Émile Masson (BEL)	+ 39' 01"

We Rode All Day

STAGE 4
BREST TO LES SABLES D'OLONNE

Jean Alavoine

The mood in here stinks. It stinks worse than Noré Barthélémy's feet. There's fleas in the bedsheets, the rain is seeping in through the roof. And while we're in the barracks out in the arse-end of Brest, the Pélissier brothers are – I don't know, I'm guessing – sleeping under Egyptian cotton bedsheets in the most expensive hotel in town, fumbling with their tiny willies as they dream of themselves.

I can't sleep. Oh, and it's morning already. So, just bollocks, basically.

Eugène hasn't slept. He was there when Pélissier told that hack from l'Auto that the other riders are all workhorses. I swear he would have swung for Henri if the gobshite hadn't ducked out of there the minute he'd said it. Dropped a bomb.

Even the Belgians are in a huff.

"Workhorses," mumbles Eugène, in between rustlings of

the morning papers.

Someone grunts back; saves me doing the job.

"Workhorses. He called us workhorses. That jumped-up, arrogant streak of fucking piss called us workhorses."

Ugh. I lift myself up off the bed, and the sheets come with me. Jesus, these sheets, we had better in the war.

"Workhorses, eh?" I fumble for my cigarettes.

"Workhorses."

A Eugène mood hangs over the room like a shit cloud. I strike a match and the first drag is always the best. Even a workhorse can appreciate the first hit of a cigarette, and this is a workhorse who can beat Henri Pélissier in a sprint. If I ever get the chance.

"Well I'm a show pony, Eugène. That would make you a stallion, and Nempon out there would be a donkey."

I always find flippancy to be the first resort. Eugène's not so convinced.

"Called him and his brother a thoroughbred. You want to let him get away with this? You think it's funny, Jean-lad?"

"Well, he is good, Eugène. He's wiping the floor with us at the moment. Him and his brother. He's been riding for the last three years, he's got the legs, he'll probably win this Tour by a full day if he carries on like this."

Eugène's fuming. "And where is the fucker anyway? Hm? I bet he didn't stay here last night.

Ah. Yes. We didn't mention that. We forgot to mention that they're staying in a nice hotel with Egyptian cotton bedsheets, and they probably got a bedtime story from Henri Desgrange, probably about ponies who travelled 300km a day and were grateful for the opportunity.

Sure, the Pélissiers are arrogant, but they're good. The public love them, they put on a show, and they're wily little sods, too. Look at Henri P – who else could get away from the front line because he was diagnosed as having a "weak disposition", and then win Paris-Roubaix AND Bordeaux-Paris? How can a man of weak disposition do night after night at the Velodrome while the rest of us are fighting the Germans?

Some men just live a charmed life. Henri Pélissier, thoroughbred indeed. He probably shits chocolate in the morning and farts perfume at night underneath a velvet duvet.

"Let's attack him," I offer. Mainly to defuse the moment, because if Eugène punches the wall of these barracks, he'll cause a draught.

"We'd have to relay for hours," mopes Christophe, the walking rulebook. Oh come on, Cri-Cri, bend the rules. Desgrange would love a proper stage to write about. Let's have some fun.

"There's a difference between a super-fast peloton and two guys relaying, Eugène. Dejo's up for it, aren't you?"

I turn to Lambot, who is seemingly lost in his thoughts. "Huh? Yeah. I'll do it."

Good man. Bring up your dead, Lambot's in town. He'll do anything to knock another rider out of the race. Any rider. Best to keep him on your team.

Eugène's turned to the race profile, thumbing his way along the route.

"Quimperle," he mutters. "That's the time and the place to do it. Just wait for a chance there. You've got 100k of flat, nothing too spiky, no big turns, and we'll have daylight. No checkpoints for 50k, so we'll have the time to put some miles on him."

The old boy's up for a bit of fun. What's more, everyone else is up for it, too.

That stringbean piece of shit won't know what's hit him.

Mischief is a marvellous incentive. You could be awake

all night. You could ride with a broken leg, but if you've got mischief on your mind, if you're doing it for fun, then you can ride for days without stopping even for a drink. It's not revenge – revenge is too dark a word, too shady a concept – it's about teaching someone a lesson. Taking someone down a peg. And why not actually try to enjoy a stage of this race for once?

Henri Pélissier

First fog, now mud. We're caked as we leave Quimper, the rain pulling at our jerseys, weighing us down, but by evening we'll have the sun for the first time this Tour and we'll dry those jerseys by the beach. Oh yes.

I, of course, will have the sun first. I'll attack in Nantes, and I shall be on average at least two degrees warmer than those peasant boys in the peloton. Soon, Francis is going to soften them up with a few attacks, we'll relay for a while so long as there are no commissioners around, and boom – off goes Pélissier number 1 , coasting into Les Sables d'Olonnes to receive the rapturous reception from his adoring crowd.

Who's your winner today? Why, Henri Pélissier, as always.

We're rolling through the hedgerows, never a good place to attack, and always a bad place for a surprise headwind. Sometimes, there is an advantage to hiding among the workhorses. Francis is shielding me from that headwind, Lambot is to my side, like a ghost, watching my every move. I'm rolling, I'm gliding, I'm effortlessly... um...

Something's not right.

I look down and check my front wheel, it seems OK,

but the machine is feeling looser, less sure of itself. The handlebars feel loose, must have been shaken up by the potholes from earlier in the stage. I'll pull over in a second. It'll be a good chance to slip my rain jacket on as well; those clouds ahead don't look good.

I zip ahead first, and pull over to the side of the road where there's a clearing. I fumble for my toolkit somewhere at the bottom of this bag. Here's the raincoat, just need to unzip this bit, so I pull at it. But as I do that, there's a shout, a cry, and three riders attack the peloton. Others follow at speed. What the…? You don't attack the race leader! Oi! GET THE FUCK BACK HERE AND WAIT FOR ME.

Francis? Where are you Francis?

"Hey, Francis? GET BACK HERE NOW!"

Fucking traitor! My own blood…

My hands are shaking. I've been tricked. They've screwed me. All this time we were coasting along, they were saving their energy for this attack.

I can't screw the headset with all this shaking. I try to get my arms into the raincoat, but it's inside out. Of course it is, it would be. And I've screwed it the wrong way, too. It's too loose. I try again, but that's not right. Why can't I do this simple fucking thing? This is costing me time; time I cannot afford to lose right now.

But Francis. My own brother. He's gone with them. Family doesn't attack family. You wait. It's the unwritten rule. Everyone waits, but above all, brothers wait.

I'm raging. Fucking raging. I tighten the headset, and I'm back on the bike. How much time have I lost now?

Route map says I've got 300km to go. That should be plenty to catch them. I just have to push. I need a push. I need dynamite. There's one pill for the stage – rations for dynamite are as low as anything else – but it won't kick in straight away. I find it, stuck in the corner of my musette, covered in crumbs from this morning's sandwich. I swallow it but I'm dry. I push a cutlet down and the last of the bidon water. It'll be, what, 20km before I feel the effects?

Lorient. Checkpoint. I don't slow down until as late as possible, wearing the brake pads with a sudden skid and the smell of burning rubber. Nice.

"How minutes many, I mean how many minutes?" Shit, I can't talk.

"5 minutes. There's 18 of them, Ficelle. They barely stopped long enough to sign their names."

He's not wrong, whoever he is. Man with moustache. These are scribbles, barely formed. We could have them for that.

"Shit. Shit Shitty Fucking Shit. Where do I sign?"

"Sign here and go. You'll get them. They're relaying, but Desgrange won't stop them, reckons it's good copy."

"Merci."

It's pretty clear that everyone in Lorient wants me to win, so with their blessing, I don't stop long. A few good lads give me a push away from the checkpoint and the whole crowd are cheering me on as I leave the town square, past the town hall, and out onto the country roads. Henri Pélissier, man of the people.

As I leave Lorient, that dynamite starts to act. My legs feel new; my lungs are capable of taking in another litre of air. My vision has improved too. That's what I love about the dynamite. Every time you take it, something new happens. Never had the vision thing before, it's like I can see round corners.

Aha, Here's old foot-monster Barthélémy himself, struggling to cope with the flat roads. I hold his wheel for a while and offer a relay, but he's not good enough.

Trouble with this boy is that he's not got the gears.

And here's the Brasier; that can only mean one thing. Desgrange. He leans out, all white moustache and red face.

"No relaying, Pélissier!"

You are fucking kidding me. Now I'm raging. "What? You let the peloton relay and not me? Do you want me to lose? Don't you want the best man to win this race?"

"They're not relaying, they're riding like true men out there. Stop relaying, stop whining, and ride like a man, Henri."

With that, he retracts his red and white face and winds up the window. Conversation over.

I look round and watch Barthélémy fade into the distance, treading water, pedalling squares. Not a nice sight. Look ahead.

Next. Here's the lad from Calais, Goethals I think his name is. He was selling socks at the start of the stage, the peasant. Look at him, it's like watching a man learning to ride a bike, swaying from side to side with his arse out of the saddle like a cyclo-tourist. There's not enough time to wheel-suck because he's slooooooow, I'm round him in a flash.

"See my socks, peasant boy?"

Haha. Another one gone. Tick.

Still no sign of that peloton, but plenty of riders are being spat out of the back. They must be going like a train.

Thud. Thud. Thud. Oh not again.

I lost concentration, found a pothole, some gravel, no doubt, and rims are hitting concrete. Back one, this time. I yank off the wheel and rip off the tyre. There's an anger to this wheel change that's making it all the more efficient. Off comes the tyre from the shoulders, give it a stretch, bang it on, pump it up. I have no nerves now. I'm left with adrenaline and dynamite, flooding my veins and I'm not shaking this time. I'm fast. I am at one with my wheel, I am the tyre, I am the rims. Pump, pump, pump, squeeze, harder please, more air. How fast am I? A record, but no one here to see it.

Shame. That would have made good copy, Desgrange.

Head down and pedal. Time is against me, so I am a man against time. One fight I'll never win, but I can try.

La Roche Bernard is up next; it's feeding time. Machurey has that smug look on his face of a man who's spent the whole day cooking. Chicken legs. Again. Cutlets. Again. A handful of baguettes, and most of it is cold.

"The food's cold, Machurey, what's wrong with you? Can't you keep it warm?"

"You're 20 minutes behind, Ficelle. You think I'm going to keep it in the oven for you? Hop along, you jumped up little man."

"20 minutes? 20 fucking minutes?" I splutter. I've lost twenty minutes and that puncture can't have been any more than five. Twenty minutes. They must be relaying, it's the only way to put 20 minutes into me while I'm riding this fast.

Machurey's enjoying this.

Insane. I stuff my pockets with everything I can before Machurey wraps his arms around the food like a protective mother. I'm out of this hole before La Roche Bernard can even notice me.

I eat, I ride, I eat, I ride. This is the monotony of the Tour lit up by the need for revenge, the need to get back into that peloton. The sun is out now, and I feel it reactivate the dynamite. Is it the dynamite or is it something else? My arms are alive again; the pain in my thighs subsides. I ride. I fly. I have to catch them.

Into the headwind I go.

We're 20km from Nantes, I calculate. Am I wrong or am I slowing down? I feel like a broken down car, the engine has started to shut down. Headlights, gone. Engine, gone. Is it the headwind? Has it blown the life out of me? Is it the dynamite? Was it not the good stuff?

Each pedal stroke feels like I'm starting afresh. I'm pedalling in squares like a sock-selling peasant from Calais. No momentum, nothing.

Worse, I feel an impulse to throw up. My mouth is dry. Such thirst. I can't go on.

And here's an incentive. There, as the roads flatten out and the landscape widens in front of me. He's there, on the horizon. He started off as a speck, but I'd know that back anywhere. The traitor. Francis, my brother, who stabbed me in the back and attacked with the peloton. Who needs dynamite when you've got a point to make? I fight the pain and reel him in, like a fisherman with the catch of his life, the one that got away, on the line.

The road widens, and I notice the gap coming down faster than it should. He's broken. I pull alongside Francis; he has tears in his eyes.

"I can't do it, Henri. I can't do it."

He looks brutal. What did they do to him? I can't let it go though.

"Why did you go? Why did you do it?"

"No helping. You know the rules. They're riding like animals. I thought I could help drag the speed down, take my turn at the front, slow it down… but they wouldn't let me."

"Who's up there? Which bastards have done this?"

"Alavoine, Christophe, couple of Belgians – Lambot, Steux, maybe Masson is in there too. They'd planned it."

"Fuck. I knew it."

"I'm going back to Paris after this. I've got nothing left. I can't ride this race any more."

Do what you want, brother. You abandoned me, I abandon you. Admire my back now.

With every pedal stroke, I put metres between myself and Francis. He really is a broken man. I need to get away from the sound of his sobbing. Oh, the thirst, though. The thirst can break a rider. I forgot to fill up my bidon in that argument with Machurey.

Oh what now? My vision, I'm riding into walls of colour. Where did they come from? Reds and greens, oh my eyes. This is a spectacle. My mouth. It's falling. Or rising. I don't know what it's doing. Froth. I'm frothing. Oh sweet froth, you'll do for a drink.

Stop this, Ficelle. Straighten up. Stop zig-zagging.

I'm hanging left. I'm falling.

I'm down. If I just stay here, if I close my eyes, maybe none of this will be happening. I'll just sleep. Sweet sleep.

Oh man, I need to drink. I scramble to my feet and fall again. What fresh hell is this?

A door. A knock. A man answers. Yes sir, today's your lucky day. Henri Pélissier it was, he knocked at your door and asked for a drink and yes, honey, I do believe he was frothing at the mouth. What did you give him? Oh, just a cognac, my dear, un 'tit cougnat, my dear, to take the edge off, cut the phlegm. It certainly seemed to livenal him up, dear. He stood right here, so he did, on this very doorstep, so he did, stood right there dripping mud onto my hydrangea, and did he look like death itself? Well I guess he did, honey, I guess he did, death stood right here on my doorstep and I gave it cognac and at least it stopped him frothing at the mouth.

I'm leaning against the wall of this house, slowly coming to. What miracle juice is this? I admire the glass, it's a good one. I asked for water, though. He gave me firewater. It burns at the back of my throat, pouring fire into every vein, shooting into my legs, my feet, my toes. I heave. A dry heave.

This is fucking stupid. Why do we do this to ourselves?

He's leaning over me, is that concern on his face? Is that what concern looks like? I guess I must look bad. I'm coming round, slowly coming round, and where am I? In an unknown man's garden, dry heaving over his flower bed, caked in mud, the veins in my head are throbbing. Look at this place. The order, the planning that must go into it, the hard work that's involved in planting, nurturing, growing, pruning… that's the trouble when you stop. You have to work with nature rather than ride as hard as you can against it. Agh, I'm going to puke.

Get me out of here. Get me back on the road.

Here we are now. Henri Pélissier is back. Fresh air makes the world of difference. I'm up to speed. I'm fast. I'm lightning fast. I'm skimming over potholes and spitting out dust. I'm burning up tyres and I'm passing traitors. The peloton has released its dead weights. The man, who was that man? What was that drink? I offered him money, he wouldn't take it.

And now Sables d'Olonnes. The saltiness is rubbing into the wounds; this is how you discover you have wounds. No place for bleeding men. I take the corners into town, each one bringing with it greater lucidity. It's funny how you can ride through anything if you have focus, if you have a single objective, if you have one thing on your mind and that one thing is catching traitors. Each corner, I take at full speed, brake first, take the racing line, inside and out – practice, practice, practice, even when you're a beaten man. You can never not get better.

The rage returns as the roads straighten up. Rage and

fatigue, a potent cocktail. These men, these workhorses, these peasants, these low-life mechanics on their cheap bikes, they took advantage of my mechanical. What glory can they take from that? And where are they now? I don't bet they haven't finished and they're already in their hotel rooms, or on the beach, or in the café, while I, the fallen thoroughbred, practice my cornering.

What was that? Was it the finishing line? Why is everyone in the road? A clamouring of arms, hands, moustaches, and as I fall, the smooth cobblestones of Sables d'Olonnes feel cold on my cheeks, my froth is filling the gaps in between the stones, I see the first drops and then I see nothing. Don't move me. Just let me lie here. Just five minutes. Just five more minutes.

Two arms, two unwelcome arms, lift me and I'm going with them. A pen. A piece of paper. Froth drips from my mouth onto the paper and a voice says don't worry, that'll do, we'll take you to your hotel room.

He's lost 35 minutes says one voice.

I'm still here, I'm still present you know. Or am I?

35 minutes is a lot, but it's not insurmountable says another. Christophe's the leader now, says the first voice, I hope he wins, I like Cri-Cri.

I'm still here. Will you stop talking about me while I'm here?

Alavoine's the one for me, says the other voice, he's a true gentleman.

And I close my eyes, and the voices fade. I feel a pillow, I feel my grey jersey fall gently to the sheets. I feel the darkness fall in on me, and my race, my Tour… it's over.

Stage 4

1	Jean Alavoine (FRA)	15h 51' 45"
2	Alfred Steux (BEL)	s.t.
3	Eugène Christophe (FRA)	s.t.
4	Émile Masson (BEL)	s.t.
5	Jacques Coomans (BEL)	s.t.
6	Léon Scieur (BEL)	+ 10' 24"
7	Firmin Lambot (BEL)	+ 13' 05"
8	Jules Masselis (BEL)	+ 31' 19"
9	Alois Verstraeten (BEL)	+ 31' 20"
10	Henri Pélissier (FRA)	+ 34' 52"

General Classification

1	Eugène Christophe (FRA)	
2	Henri Pélissier (FRA)	+ 11' 42"
3	Émile Masson (BEL)	+ 15' 51"

STAGE 5
SABLES D'OLONNES TO BAYONNE

Firmin Lambot

It's so dark, I can't count the riders. 16 or 17? I'm pretty sure they're not here.

"Léon, can you see them?"

He's craning his neck as well. Still no Pélissiers.

"I told you," he smiles. "Definitely gone."

You always doubt, you always think – well maybe they'll return. Maybe they didn't catch that train. And you'd turn up at the café and Henri would be there, strutting around, reminding everyone how he won Paris-Roubaix, the toughest race of them all, and we all know he was higher than a kite that day and he'll be higher than a kite today, just to rub it in.

There's nothing wrong with drugs per se. Racing is 14 hours of relentless shitshow, and most riders don't earn much. You take drugs to get to the end of the day, even if it means you cross the line babbling like a baby – you made it to the end and you fight another day. That's why riders take pills and supplements. It's why some riders drink like fish. To cross the line.

But a natural talent like Pélissier. He could beat us most days on water and biscuits while we're on the rocket fuel. And I'm glad he's not here – because even if we're denied the greater glory of winning a Tour with Pélissier in it, we don't have to put up with his gloating and sniping.

That changes everything. We're all reviewing our race strategies, revising our views of each other. Christophe and Masson lead the race, although nobody thinks Masson has it in him, and Christophe – he's gritty. A tough old veteran of the pre-war Tours… hang on, aren't we all?

We're all reviewing this stage, too. Léon's been more nervous about this stage than any of the mountain stages. Boring racing is dangerous, he says. And this will be a long, drawn-out, uneventful roll into Bayonne from 17 pairs of tired legs. It won't be a stage for attacks, or running someone into the ground, it'll be a stage for holding yourself back. Saving energy.

We're a silent peloton, on the outskirts of Sables d'Olonnes, huddled together in a vow of cycling silence. Every man knows this is going to bore us to death, and no one has any solution to that, no one has the legs to liven it up.

On a day like today, you save yourself. You measure every last drop of energy you have, and you carefully assess every possible drop of energy you can get back.

How are we going to get through this?

Food

For every 50km, you need at least one baguette sandwich. So that's eight. I have carefully portioned them out – in the morning, two jam sandwiches for breakfast, followed by cheese sandwiches for the afternoon and back to jam in the late afternoon because you need the sugar.

Warning to all amateur riders who fancy themselves endurance athletes – do not drink water other than to rinse out the dirt from your mouth. Look at young Honoré Barthélémy, vomiting by the side of the road. Why so? Because he drank water. If you want to go long stages, hold off from the drinking, and just eat loads. And those riders who think alcohol is going to stave off the pain? Ever seen one of them win? No, I didn't think so.

Chat

Carefully portion out your chat, too. You have spent the last week with these men, including the days off, so there is very little left to say that hasn't already been said. However, talking does help alleviate some of the pain and the boredom of a transitional stage like this. But save your conversations for the late morning and early afternoon where the peloton slows down and you don't have to concentrate too hard due to a) darkness or b) proper racing.

Toilet breaks

All riders need a dump. I bet you hadn't thought about that – or you didn't want to think about it – but dumping is strategic. On most stages, you're too busy racing or climbing, but on slow, dull stages like this, you're constantly thinking about loo breaks.

So on the evening before you start racing, eat well and have your dump just before the départ. This ensures that you will get through the hours of darkness and your first few sandwiches with nothing in the tank, so to speak.

However, the more you eat, the more you'll need to evacuate, so timing is everything.

You'll essentially be looking for a single-dump stage. Two dumps can be fatal, as other riders may attack mid-dump. Three dumps, and frankly, you're out of the race. You might as well puncture. So on this stage, I have calculated that I should dump at approximately 1 o'clock, just before the feeding station, unless there is an attack on and I need to cover it. This implies that the sandwiches must equally be timed, and you should always double check the food that comes out of Machurey's feeding stations. Paul Duboc won't touch any of it – he prepares everything himself, claims they're all trying to poison him.

Wee breaks have to be quick and efficient. Of course. But if you're not taking on too much water, you should be fine. Weeing yourself on the stage is viewed as generally acceptable in race situations, but on a stage like today, it would imply that you're desperate, hanging on, and that you're prey for someone to attack. There's nothing more obvious than the smell of wee.

Effort

Another factor that has to be carefully apportioned is your effort. Pedalling all day when you have an objective – climbing a mountain, slaying a Pélissier, chasing a breakaway – it comes easy. And it comes easy because you're not thinking about it. On these stages, sans objectif, you are conscious of every pedal stroke.

Now, I'm using my Christophes, some of the boys prefer to call them foot holders, but Eugène invented them, he deserves the credit. This means that I am able to use my up-stroke on the pedal as well as the down-stroke. No small thing, I'll tell you, it allows you to spread the effort out. Rather than pushing with all your might left-right, left-right, you can apportion the effort equally between the up-stroke and the down-stroke, and maintain an adequate speed.

Naturally, we will be using less effort today, as our effort needs to be held in reserve for the mountains, but every pedal stroke is enough to add an inch to each mountain unless you measure it responsibly.

I'll be frank with you. I have absolutely no idea where we are, or how far we have to go. What I do know is that the sandwiches are depleted, the pace has increased every so slightly, and the sun is shining. The actual sun. Funny, it could have been shining for the last three hours, but now I'm riding into some form and some fitness, I'm able to switch my mind off and just ride, oblivious to my surroundings. I'm sure Alavoine is talking to me, or he was, maybe I appear rude or unconcerned.

If you start picturing the finish town too soon, you're cooked. I try to picture the next big town, and ride small stages from one to the next. Checkpoints and feeding stations help. From there, you start again, one small race to the next. This stage probably has eight smaller stages within it.

It's going to be a long day.

Léon Scieur

I have found over my years of riding these races that a rider has three factors he can control. One, the bike. Two, the body. Three, the mind.

Now, the bike is what it is. If you're like Eugène Christophe or Firmin Lambot, your bike is well-oiled and very much tinkered-with. Mine is loved, if a little worn.

The body and the mind, alas, are less easy to control. There are days, like today, when the body is not up to the job. This is where the mind needs to step in and 'up its game', so to speak. My body, it is fair to say, has failed me today. I woke up early this afternoon with legs like two sacks of wheat. Unmoving and heavy. I pottered around the hotel room, trying to shake some kind of life into them, but the writing was already on the wall. I went through all three of the masseurs without any luck.

Today would not be a 'body first' kind of a day.

Which means that the mind – the spirit – has to intervene. This stage is long, an awful, transitional, long drag towards the mountains, that could have been avoided by taking the train during the rest day, but formalities are what formalities are, and the stage towns need their stages. Therefore, we are faced with an interminably boring, flat stage that will probably take us all of 16 hours, and I have two legs that can barely take me up a flight of stairs, never mind cycle over 400km.

To stimulate the body, the mind must remain active, and it must either convince the body that there is some lifeblood that can be circulated (in this case, it can absolutely not), or it must fool the body into forgetting about the lack of thrust. Today, therefore, I have to ride with my mind. And to the public, the throngs of humanity that line the streets like besuited hedgerows, I am on my own. To my over-active mind, I am riding with ghosts.

First, I am shamelessly sucking the wheel of the much-regretted Marcel Kerff. Marcel, I cry, pedal harder, we're falling backwards, and his sepia outline turns and smiles that smile of his, old Marcel, ever the servant, my inspiration and my guide.

Why did you have to be so curious, Marcel?

Bends, slaloms and curves, an unusual turn on this otherwise straight, nonsensical stage, and Marcel shifts to protect me from the sea breeze that laps in from the Atlantic. As he peels off, his job done, Lucien Mazan, the man we knew as Petit-Breton, falls in alongside me. Lucien, the dapper, debonair Argentinian, you could have been here, Lucien, you shouldn't have died.

He knows. He nods. A drunk driver. Of all the ways to go. Of all the stupid, inhumane, mad fucking ways to die, a drunk driver.

There's a gradient coming up and Lucien goes ahead, it's steeper than I'd thought, steeper than he'd thought; he's out of breath by the time we coast so I offer him my wheel and we ride down through the outskirts of Bordeaux. Lucien would have appreciated a stop-off at one of the chateaux, perhaps we should do that, Lucien, or we could stop off and steal some grapes.

Perhaps we should. Like the old days.

Lucien is joined by Octave Lapize, Octave, dear old Octave, dear misunderstood Octave, died a hero's death so he did, or so they say, no one ever knows quite how anyone really passed, but word is that Octave was shot down in the east, and died in hospital. Octave acknowledges this with a smile and offers me his wheel. The roads are wider around here; the heat is ratcheting up with every bike length, but Octave has a spare bidon for me, something I'm confident Henri Desgrange wouldn't mind, as it's Octave, that is.

We ride on in silence. Me and my ghosts.

For a moment I'm alone; who's this in the distance? It's my father, cheering me on from the side of the road, halfway between ditch and vineyard, "Allez Léon", he's screaming, as if he ever screamed that while he was alive.

Father who hated the bicycle, that wretched invention

that took his son to neighbouring towns that were out of bounds to men, that satanic machine that broadened horizons, oh how I wanted to show you otherwise, father, how I needed to show you there's a career in this, there's a life beyond the glass blowing factories of Florennes. There's a life beyond the cobblestones and the grey shitty skies, just look up and look around you father, see where we are and how far we've come.

When I brought home my first bicycle, he threw it out onto the pavement, and screamed at me never to bring that contraption into his home. I cried for weeks on end. I'd saved for that bicycle, every day putting aside a few more centimes here, and a few more centimes there. I kept it at a friend's house, and went to polish it every night, cleaning the chain, oiling the nuts and bolts, buffing the saddle. I learned gearing before many other boys learned how to turn the wheels and balance themselves. And I swore that day, as I did on many occasions afterwards, that the bicycle would become my life and I would devote myself to a career on two wheels, and I look up and he's gone, or I'm gone and he's far behind me, so now he knows, now he can see and now the body remembers what the body can do. Ah yes, father, I forgot to tell you that I don't just cycle from Florennes to the factory, I had this mad idea to cycle 5,500km around France for money, quite a lot of it, in fact.

So father, look at me now. I've cycled from Belgium to Bayonne, I'm racked with pain and my legs have failed me. But if you gave me one thing, it's spirit.

Machurey

Old Henri wouldn't know half of what happens in his Tour, not that he's got the time to think about us functionaries and our goings-on. But when this Tour is done, I'll be making a trip back to Labouheyre, so I will, if Miss Henriette will have me. And I hope she will, if I may be so bold.

Oh Maurice, control yourself.

Where do I start? Oh, at the beginning, as I always must. You see, we'd arrived yesterday evening at the Hotel des Voyageurs, which is ever so appropriate given that we are Voyageurs ourselves. Old Madame Lassus was there to welcome us, just like in the years before the war as she always did. Use this, use that, don't use this, don't touch that, keep your hands off my pots and pans, and if you want any goose fat well there's a man down the road but don't think he's got any for you cyclist types. And off she went, slamming the door behind her. Well I never, I said to young Tisserang, the baby-faced reporter boy, you'd better go get some goose fat, hadn't you.

So there I was, pottering around with the pots and pans when Miss Henriette walked in to the kitchens, oh she was a vision I tell you; I was quite knocked back. A lovely sweet face, blue eyes and that dark hair that you find down here, it's almost Spanish but they're not so fiery or temperamental, won't have your eye out in a fight. Can I help you sir, she asked, and I melted like the butter in a frying pan, so I did, I was all fluttery.

Y-ye-yes, I be-bel-believe you can, Madame.

Madamoiselle.

Oh, if you are to be corrected by a lady, let it be this way. Shall I show you how we roast a duck round these parts?

Oh I, I'd, I'd be de-del-delighted.

Oh Maurice, how you stumble in front of a lady.

Tisserang burst in at that point, there's no goose fat sir, what are we going to do? But Miss Henriette had a solution, and off she popped and back she popped in next to no time, arms laden.

You'll need plenty of this, sirs, and I sent Tisserang on another shopping expedition, just to get him out of the way. Find a farmer, one far away from here, and come back later, much later; in fact, don't bother coming back - just take the night off, there's a good boy. I didn't say that. Or did I? I really lost track of my mind.

So I made the food for the riders, and Miss Henriette made us a magret de canard with Landaises potatoes and brought out a petit Cotes de Blaye from before the war. 1912, I nodded approvingly, that was a good year, a very good year indeed. They all were before the fighting started.

And what can a man say other than the magret was impeccable, the wine sumptuous and the company... divine. Miss Henriette, she asked about the riders, asked if Mr Christophe was going to win the Tour or whether a Belgian rider might win it. Well I was quite taken aback, a lady with intimate knowledge of the Tour; how times have changed since we came back from the war.

She asked about my work, and how on earth do I manage in the north or in the east? How do I manage, I replied, sometimes I have to rely on the goodness of the locals like yourself, Miss Henriette. I do swear she blushed at that, and we washed up together, well I dried and she washed and then she bade her farewell, said she had chores to do, and I said I had mine as well, nodding down at the supplies she had kindly brought.

And now, as the sunshine worms its way into my skin

still soaked with the rain from the north, I'm standing here a day later, dreaming of Miss Henriette and a life here in the South-West, rearing ducks and deep-frying potatoes for dinner while Miss Henriette picks herbs from the garden underneath the evening sunshine.

Maurice. Snap out of it.

A support car flashes by. That's no one important, I make a note. Wait for the telegram. I glance down at yesterday's l'Auto. They should be near Bordeaux by now. I should be with Miss Henriette by now.

Maurice. Wake up.

Another support car. Did I get the time wrong? There's Desmarets, getting out of the car and pushing one fat leg in front of the other. That's the thing about Bob; everything he does is like he's trying to imitate other human beings. Even walking seems to be a mickey-take.

"Ten minutes, Machurey, I hope you're ready."

"Of course I'm bloody ready, Bob. And get your fat fingers off the food, none of it's for you."

"Oh come on Maurice, you didn't save us some duck?"

Duck? How could he have known about the magret? The stolen moments with Miss Henriette.

"Duck? Erm… how could… there's no duck… I mean…"

"Relax, Maurice, we didn't expect you to find duck in these conditions. I'm surprised you found anything in this dump," he sneers, surveying the town centre with disdain. You leave Labouheyre alone, Desmarets, keep your fat face out of here.

And then a clatter as a rider crashes straight into the table, sending platters and plates scrambling for the table edge. It's Duboc, the farmer from Normandy. Thankfully he's not broken anything, and now he's inspecting the food, so he is, all tiny-eyed and suspicious.

"What's this?" he enquires, picking up a chicken leg and

squinting at it.

"It's a badger's anus, Duboc, what do you think it is?"

"Don't piss around with me, Machurey, what kind of chicken is it?"

"A local chicken," I shrug. I tried one for breakfast; it's actually rather good, I might take one with me tomorrow.

"Eat it for me, then," he retorts, shoving the chicken leg back at me.

"Are you bloody kidding me? Eat it, Duboc, you fool, you're lucky to get anything."

"Look, just nibble at it – prove to me you've not poisoned it. Go on."

How dare he! To accuse me of poisoning the riders of the Tour de France! What a horrible little man.

Lambot and Alavoine roll in next at what seems to be an excessively leisurely pace, and both seem surprised that Duboc is here before them. Once Duboc sees them tearing into the chicken legs, he sniffs and starts stuffing them into his musette. If it's good enough for them, eh.

"Not long to go, lads," I encourage them, but I'm not in their world, as they exchange jibes with Duboc. A couple of lads are smoking, one's got his flask out, the Calais boy Goethals I think his name is, he thinks he can drink his way through the stage. Coomans has lit his pipe, the odour is wafting over the table. Cherry. I wonder how riders make it through days like this without going insane, 400 kilometers of flat roads, with just food, drink, and a smoke to get them through to Bayonne where they'll probably be all together again, no time differences.

Duboc has gone, chicken legs strewn across the town square. Lambot and Alavoine are quickly on to him, and Mr Christophe is on to them as well. Masson and Chassot are still stuffing their musettes, oblivious to the race.

And before long, even the stragglers have been and gone.

Barthélémy, the boy who started off so bright-eyed, and now looks like a hollowed-out shell of a man, he takes what's left and slumps into the corner, staring into the distance. What have we done to him?

I stare into the distance, too. Dreaming of Miss Henriette, and the magret de canard, and of how a lady can take an interest in this ridiculous race and how a man can find that charming, and how times change and how if they keep changing, I'll come back to Labouheyre to find Miss Henriette, and I'll stop circling this country one year this way, one year that way, and I'll settle here, selling duck eggs by the roadside while she cooks my dinner for me. There will be seasons in Labouheyre, not just dusty summers where the air hangs still, but Miss Henriette will show me how to get ready for winter, which is always colder than you think it will be – microclimate - and we'll welcome the first burst of spring as she tells me which flowers come first, which ones come last. We'll watch the vegetable patches bloom into life as the surprise of summer creeps up on us, pretending it will never end, promising the world as cycle races flash by, wasps live and die, the autumn blows in, and still I'll be here with Miss Henriette as we watch the leaves fall, just us and the world around us, a never-ending cycle of life and death and rebirth, but all in one place, and all in each others' arms.

Jean Alavoine

Hey ho, what's this? Duboc is here before us!

"Hey Lambot – did you know Duboc was ahead of us?"

He shrugs, maybe he did. Maybe he didn't. How did I not know?

"Oi, apple boy. What's up with the chicken?"

He holds it up like an oily rag. "Look at it – Machurey's trying to poison me, I tell you, it's a funny colour."

"Ha you twerp Duboc, it's a well-fed chicken. Not like your Normandy chickens who get blotto on your dodgy fermented apples."

Lambot likes that one. "Tell him Machurey's pissed in his bidon."

Duboc doesn't like this constant jibing, but he made his bed, he has to lie in it.

I stuff a few more cutlets into the bag – there's only 50km to go, so any more food will probably lie heavy, so let's call it a post-ride meal. Funny place to have a feeding station.

Off goes Duboc. I shout out to Lambot – "you coming?"

He's onto him, and so am I, and we're out of this nowhere town, on the road to Bayonne. Christophe's looming behind, with about six or seven others on his tail, the dreaded peloton, a horde of bores, dulled by a day's dozing on their bikes.

What if I close my eyes? Perhaps I can ride to Bayonne without having to chew the fat with dullards like Coomans if I've got my eyes closed. I try it, only to be jerked back into line by the boy Lucotti who has appeared from nowhere, or maybe he was always there.

"Stay with it, boys," shouts Christophe, warming to his role as race leader.

For once, I have nothing funny to say.

I feel an alcoholic waft to my right. It's Masson.

"Cognac?" he offers his hip flask.

"Mm, why not," and I swig back a healthy mouthful and feel it burn the back of my throat. "What sort of cognac was that?"

He laughs and has another swig himself. "Origin

unknown."

"Then it can't be cognac, can it?"

We're hardly going at a lick. I've got time to pull out a pre-rolled cigarette, light it, ride with no hands for about a hundred metres, and smoke it to the quick. This is a shit stage and we're all feeling it. We're all feeling the pain of putting the Pélissiers to the sword, but we're feeling the boredom, the aches and the torpor of hours and hours in the saddle doing nothing of interest.

That cigarette has really opened up the lungs, though. I usually save them for just before a climb, but we've got an uphill finish as I remember it, and that's all I need as we enter Bayonne through the back streets.

I remember this place now, there's a swing left, and a swing right – get yourself in line and then you're up towards the citadelle. Okey dokes, who's coming with me?

"Chassot – you up for a ride? Hm?"

He is, good boy. Who else is coming? Oh, all the Belgians! Well, hello boys. Time to ride.

I attack first, Chassot second, and we've got Coomans with his pipe hanging out of his back pocket, massive legs pumping away at his pedals, he'll not get far riding like that. Forget Coomans, focus on Chassot, he's a wily customer. Scieur now has a pop, this guy is no sprinter but he's relentless. If that's his pace all the way to the finish, I'll mop him up before the line, he has no acceleration.

In fact, Scieur's the one to latch on to. Here comes the incline, let's watch them drop away. Christophe's gone, fired out the back. Masson and Lambot have gone, too – now the climb is starting to tell. Why didn't we just ride around Bayonne all day? This is fun.

Chassot makes another move – feisty. I like this. I swing round from Scieur's wheel to his, we've got under a hundred metres; I have to make my move soon.

90 metres. Wait.

80 metres. Think about it.

70 metres. Wait for him. Wait…

60 metres. Still waiting.

50. 40.

30 metres – he looks round. Idiot – now I slam my thighs down, powering down into the pedal through my calves, into my feet, every wheel length takes me closer to Chassot, alongside him.

20 metres – he knows he's lost it, you can never beat a man coming round you, he'll always have the acceleration. I'm that man.

10 metres – anyone going to take this from me?

Didn't think so. Alavoine takes Bayonne.

Chassot slaps me on the back. I like a competitor who acknowledges his victor, so I slap him back on his, and we exchange pleasantries. Maybe I'll share my bonus with him, for making a shit stage so enjoyable at the close.

Now, let's get the formalities out of the way. I want to get back to Pano the masseur, so I need to find Desgrange. Where is the old boy?

I dump my bike and push through the oncoming crowd, all cheap suit and cheap booze, and there in the middle of it all is Desgrange, pen and pad in hand, ready for an Alavoine monologue to fill his column tomorrow.

"Ready Desgrange? Right, get this down, I don't want you hanging around too long so let's get the interview out of the way eh."

Set the marker down early, that's the only way to deal with Desgrange.

"You'll be seeing a lot of me if I keep winning these stages, Henri. How am I feeling? I'm feeling just fine and dandy, as good as you can be after five brutal stages like that, and I reckon I've got plenty left in me for the

Pyrenees tomorrow."

He asks something about today's stage. Do I tell him it was a pile of shit? Maybe not.

"I wasn't keen on the fog last night, it was like riding through cotton wool. The rest of the stage? Bof. Interview over, I'm off to see Pano."

Stage 5

1	Jean Alavoine (FRA)	18h 54' 07"
2	René Chassot (FRA)	s.t.
3	Léon Scieur (BEL)	s.t.
4	Joseph Van Daele (BEL)	s.t.
5	Jacques Coomans (BEL)	s.t.
6	Alois Verstraeten (BEL)	s.t.
7	Luigi Lucotti (ITA)	s.t.
8	Eugène Christophe (FRA)	+ 13"
9	Émile Masson (BEL)	s.t.
10	Firmin Lambot (BEL)	s.t.

General Classification

1	Eugène Christophe (FRA)	
2	Émile Masson (BEL)	+ 15' 51"
3	Firmin Lambot (BEL)	+ 49' 49"

STAGE 6
BAYONNE TO LUCHON

Jean Alavoine

There are a few boys here who haven't been to the mountains before. Honoré Barthélémy, for instance, says he's never even climbed a mountain in his life. Not even so much as a hill.

He almost craps himself when I read what Henri has prepared for us in l'Auto this morning.

"Honoré, listen to this… courtesy of Papa Desgrange over there, right… ready? The riders are asked to take extra care in the mountains. There are a large number of horses, donkeys, mules, cows, bulls, calves, goats, sheep and pigs in the mountain that are likely to wander into your path at any stage. Take particular care when going down the many windy descents."

He's gone white. Hilarious.

"Wait, there's more… 6th stage, blah blah blah. 7th stage, blah blah. Mountain roads are narrow and badly maintained. Some of them have deep ravines. The ground is badly broken up. Descending is dangerous for anyone not taking particular care. Rocks, precipices, blah blah blah. Come on Desgrange, get to the good bit…"

"Ah yes, bears. There are bears in the Pyrenees, and if you see one, don't shit yourself as they follow the scent."

"It does NOT say that, Mr Alavoine!" he jumps up and tries to take the newspaper. I jump away and he chases me, trying to snatch at the yellow rag.

Eugène's enjoying this.

"Tell him about the wolves, Jean-boy," he shouts out.

"Ah yes, the wolves. It says try not to brake too hard because they mistake the sound of brakes on rims for a mate and they'll try to hump you."

Ah come on Honoré. Join in the fun. I put my arm round him.

"Tell you what, if there is a bear, Old Eugène over here, right – he used to ride when they had guns, so he's probably got his pistol in his musette there."

"Never leaves my side," he smiles.

"Told you so. You see a bear, just let Eugène know and he'll sort you out."

Every rider fears something. Some fear bears, others fear the ravines. I fear the climb itself. I fancy a mountain stage this year, I think I've got the legs, but it's not until you've crested the first peak that you believe you can do it. It's been 5 years since any of us took on a mountain.

Fear can do one of two things. It can freeze you to the spot, or it can push you over the top. I've seen men fall apart at the sight of a mountain, and I've seen others grit their teeth and take their fear on like a boxer coming out of his corner against a man ten times his size.

"Tell you what Honoré, if you follow me up the mountain, I'll hang back for you, what do you say? We'll take on the first two together."

"I like the sound of that, Mr Alavoine," he beams, and

he's positively wide-eyed.

150km

What has Barthélémy been eating? Or drinking? For the last week and a half, nobody has seen him and now we're all marvelling at his rear end.

You know, there was a time when standing on your pedals was The. Wrong. Thing. To. Do. Leave it to the ladies, they'd say. Stay seated, let your calves do the work, never – I repeat, never – get out of the saddle.

But look at Barthélémy dancing on his pedals. He's balletic.

If you'd ever seen Garrigou at his peak, you'd know what I mean. At his best, the Cypriot was the finest climber the world had ever seen, not that the world had seen many climbers, but you know what I mean. Remember when Lapize called the race organisers criminals? Garrigou was streaking up the Tourmalet with an ice cream in his left hand, and a blonde on his knee. Probably.

He made it look easy, but he never got out of his saddle. Old Gustave was graceful in his own way, but not in a Barthélémy way. As graceful as a pre-war man could have been.

They say that in 1911, he poisoned Duboc. That's when Duboc was popular, now he's just a grumpy orchard farmer from the past, and the fans back then wanted Garrigou's blood. I don't know if he really did try to poison Duboc, but anything went in those early tours. The riders were rough and the crowds were wild. Proper wild. So to get him through Rouen, they offered to disguise him. Desgrange gave him a choice of three wigs, but he went out and found his own hairpiece. Disguise me if you will, he said, but at the very least make me look good.

Thing is, you can't hide a rider like Gustave. Especially when he's wearing the most elaborate wig in the shop.

So they tried to hide him. Surrounded him with cars, paid off other riders to huddle around him in an impromptu peloton. The fans came with their rotten fruit, ready to hurl all manner of abuse at the man, but they went home in awe.

The Cypriot, they said, he glided through our town like an angel.

They still never forgave him for the Duboc incident, though.

I turn to Lambot.

"Oi, Lambot. Reckon you can climb like that?"

A shake of the head. Not even Lambot, the hero of 1914, can keep up with this guy. It won't be long before he's busted us all, but we hang on for the show. Up he goes, attack after attack, this guy's fucking amazing. He's attacking nobody, just putting on acceleration after acceleration for the fun of it. Burst upon burst, and each one more balletic than the last.

It really is a thing of beauty, so long as you can hang on to see it. A gentle sway from left to right, right to left, man and machine in perfect harmony. Such power, and such little effort. Honoré is making these roads look like sweet, sweet concrete. I watch the lull of baguettes in his back pocket, the musette's movements in perfect time with each push of the pedal.

"Forget it, Jean-boy. We're wasting our time here. Let him go."

"Gustave wouldn't have given up like that."

He looks genuinely confused. "What?"

"Garrigou. Gustave Garrigou, he wouldn't give up chasing him."

"Yes he would. He'd say leave it – fight another day. Let

him go."

I concede. I suck in the thinning air, and return to my plight. My own race today is about getting home in one piece. No bears, no wolves, just reaching the top of the Peyresourde, the Tourmalet, and the others, whether I'm graceful or not.

Maybe I'll get out of the saddle, too.

Firmin Lambot

If you want to ride a bike, you have to know how to read a man.

This morning, I read Christophe's face. I read his gestures, the nervous taps on the handlebars, the unusually lengthy preparation before the off. The lack of chatter and bonhomie, the focus on his little rituals...

And that's how I knew I had to attack. A distracted rider is easy to pick off, because he doesn't know. He doesn't see you; he only sees the road in front of him. He's blind to attacks, and that's a weakness you have to exploit.

Occasionally, you turn, because you have to know. Is he close? Is he closing in?

Why is he nowhere?

Eugène Christophe

Some days, I hate racing. I hate the bike, I hate the shitshow spectacle, I hate Desgrange, I hate the boredom. I hate stages like the last one, a pancake-flat, boring transitional, climb-less, arse-numbing fucking waste of time that does nobody any good. It's the same every year. You ride for 400km, and at the end, Jean Alavoine wins.

And some days, I fear racing. I don't hate the Tourmalet. I fear it. The wrong turn. The broken forks. The longest walk. There isn't a single rider who would have woken up today with a spring in his step. We've ridden all this way, drawing the mountains closer with each pedal stroke until they rise up into view, pulling themselves into the sky and taunting us, as if to say "we've been here millennia and you think you can conquer us?"

Perhaps I can't, but I know a blacksmith who can help.

The days are long gone since cycling was seen as a death sport, but the Tourmalet, the Peyresourde and the Aspin are three climbs that could end your life in any number of ways. And who's closer to death than the old man himself, the old Gaul, Eugène.

You could die of a heart attack on the way up. The air is thinner, and some men smoke to clear the lungs. They are idiots. Cigarettes won't help you up here. You need to sit back, broaden the shoulders and breathe deep. Follow the goat paths and use your cyclocross skills.

You could die by falling into a ravine. Descending is technical, and every rider has his own technique. I used to ride with one rider who got off his bike at every hairpin. He didn't last long.

You could be killed by a bear. Nobody has been killed by a bear, but Henri persists in publishing the same warning day after day – watch out for the bears. And the wolves. And the random animals walking in your path. The amateurs of the day back in the first Tours, they'd race with guns in their musettes. It added to the air of menace – you could end up a snack for a grizzly bear, but you could also end up shot dead by Maurice Garin, the man who had to win at all costs.

It crossed your mind with every attack. If he can't keep up, would it cross his mind to shoot you? At least aim for the feet, or the tyres. Garin was one of the first of the true athletes, and he'd have won regardless, but his gun gave him a mental edge over the gun-less.

But first the climb, and our first taste of real pain.

Climbing is all about cadence. A constant, measurable 1, 2, 3, 4, 5, 6, 7, 8 that you tap out with your pedals like the conductor of an orchestra. You must find cadence before pain finds you, so you strike up the orchestra at the first sign of a gradient, and hope the metronomic beat of your feet can hold its rhythm. The Osquich is the first climb of the day. There are stretches here that should be taken by foot – not suitable for skinny wheels – but re-mounting is a nightmare, and you need a push. The French riders get a push, you can guess what happens to the Belgians.

Talking of whom, I'm riding today with Scieur and Masson. I like Scieur, he's a good man. He comes across all gentle and grandfathery, not bad for a man in his 30s. He'll spend years bouncing grandchildren on his knee, telling them stories of how great Eugène Christophe was, and that belies the competitive streak in him. He's a locomotive. Not much acceleration, but when he goes, he keeps on going and he's impossible to shake off on his day.

Today, Léon has been having a bit of fun, and has blown himself out. He's practically wheezing as he hangs on to my wheel at the foot of the Aubisque. Masson has that "kill me now" look on his face, and we're only entering the first climb of four.

"Léon, how's the legs?" I shout behind me.

"Ask me in 10 miles, Cri-Cri," he pants.

Concentrate now, Eugène. 1, 2, 3, 4, 5, 6, 7, 8. Every stroke, measured equally, a dose of power poured out meticulously equal to the previous dose, knowing that you only have so much to give to the mountain. Let the orchestra play.

And here comes the pain. Cadence, Eugène. Control it, don't let the gradient alter the rhythm. Pain shifts as you climb, it moves from ribs to rump, from head to toe, and you try to master it mentally, you think to yourself that Barthélémy, the boy with the ingrown toenail, is probably 5km ahead, on his way down the mountain, and you say 'there's a man who knows how to master pain'.

Léon's off again, powering past me, out of the saddle and pumping at his pedals. From nowhere, Lucotti shoots past as well. Cat and mouse.

Ignore them.

I hear my breath. The shorter it gets, the louder it becomes.

I feel heat rising to my head. Why didn't I get that haircut? I stoop low over the handlebars to get air to my head but it breaks my cadence and I have to start again at 1. The audience groans. The conductor has dropped his baton.

Here's Léon again.

"What are you playing at?" I scream as I pull alongside, spit flickering behind me.

"Don't tell me this isn't fun, Cri-Cri!", he beams, and with that, he's gone again, Lucotti in hot pursuit. "Va f'an culo, l'Italiano" he screams as Lucotti hollers "che chazzo" at Léon's disappearing back.

The beginning of a beautiful friendship?

I smile at the thought, and I realise it's the first time I've smiled on a bike this Tour. Perhaps I'm having fun, too? Once the pain is pushed to the background, once you accept it and welcome it, you enter a different phase. You almost welcome the mountain.

I've reached the top of the Aubisque, and before me,

there she is. The wrong turn. Green with menace, the Tourmalet. She's been waiting patiently, waiting for her turn. Six years she has waited for me, six years, brooding silently for the man with the broken machine.

Sinewy paths are scattered along her back, where walkers and cyclists seek easier gradients. The Tourmalet is a thing of beauty, from a distance, but she taunts me. She haunts me. As I descend the Aubisque, I keep my eye on her.

When I start the climb, she caresses me upwards, for that's what the Tourmalet does; she lures you into a false sense of security. The more aware among us would notice that today, the temperature is dropping quicker than usual, but she doesn't mention that as you climb, maintaining your cadence for the orchestra inside. No, she fails to inform you that today, she's snow-capped. Another trick up her sleeve.

You may have thought that she's helping you. Easing her gradients as you pump at the pedals, flattening herself out and bouncing you up over easy steps, the siren calling out to sailors. Come this way, I promise so much.

The paths widen, the breeze whips up behind you, the Tourmalet pretends to be your friend. As the mercury drops, the crowds thin, and a handful of hardy climbers beckon you forward and you notice that but for them, you are alone. Just you and her.

And then... the magic is gone. She has lulled you in, and you – the rider, seduced by the song of the siren – you realise you are in a trap. I skid on some compacted snow, regain my composure, and plough forward, only to hit another gradient that no bicycle can handle. 20% perhaps? I dismount, and push forward, but the snow is seeping into my shoes. I hate the wet. Fuck. I remount and push down onto the pedals with straight legs, each push a minor revolution of the wheel. I look back, I look ahead, still nobody around. Just me and her.

I glance down at my forks. Still intact. It was right here, six years ago, right at this very point, with a ravine to my left, with a stone wall to my right, that the bike gave way, and my nightmare began. A stone jumps up at me, hits me on the chin. Another bounces off the frame of the bike.

But the bike holds. And who would have thought this raggedy old crockpot would hold. A standard-issue, gun-metal grey Peugeot, known for its suspect forks, has made it past the top of the Tourmalet, and I could kiss it. I could embrace it. And in the distance, I hear her, pounding the earth in frustration, because she failed. This old bike made it through the worst, and as the gradients turn negative, it's holding still. A good bike will see you through summers and winters, but this one has seen through the Tourmalet's worst.

Time to descend. I take yesterday's newspaper out of my musette and shove it down my jersey. I pull the hat down over my ears and beat my hands on the handlebars, trying to circulate the blood. Time to leave her, and at speed. I pedal as hard as I can down the mountainside, taking each hairpin at breakneck speed. The faster I get away from her, the less chance she has of catching me. Her chances recede as I slalom down her side. What tricks await? Will she lash out her tail?

At speed, the descent is like any other. I remember the girl in the gingham dress, she must have been here, on my left. There's Elie Bède's house, his daughters will be inside, probably unaware of my passing. Here's Sainte-Marie-de-Campan, whose cobblestones I have marked in my mind forever. There's smoke rising from the forge, but it's not for me. I lost several hours here six years ago.

Today, I barely have time to smell the smoke.

The final hairpin. I nearly come off, the back wheel slashing out at an angle, but I revive myself, find my composure, and spring away in a sprint. There is an imaginary line at the end of each mountain, where the mountain itself ends and the valley begins. I imagine I have crossed it, and the Tourmalet rues its chances. For another year, at least.

Honoré Barthélémy

This is it. This is Luchon. My heart is pounding, Am I ten seconds ahead or am I ten minutes ahead? I look round.

Still no one. Ah man, come on. There hasn't been anyone for hours, but I keep looking.

Swing – a cobbled corner. Swing – a smoother one. Left, then right.

Right, then left. And now people, shit man loads of people, loads of grey, loads of screaming faces, woosh, they're gone. Focus on your race, Noré, focus. Head down.

Shall I look around? One last peep?

No. Head down. And here it comes. The line, the banner, and woah have I done it? The crowd are enclosing on me, have I finished? Am I done now? Is that it? Is this what it's like to win a stage?

I'm being proper mobbed down here. Fuzzy men with fuzzy suits are trying to grab a piece of me, like I'm some kind of hero. It's all arms and pats on the back and hugs that I don't want. Hugs that they really shouldn't want, either. Really, gents, I'm a roadie who's been over a few mountains. I've weed myself twice, I'm sweating like a pig and I'm dustier than a chimney sweep. You really don't want to hug me right now. You might catch something.

I think I won the stage. Was I fast? Still no one has followed me home. They'll be a long time, the crowd says. They'll be a long, long time. I wasn't meant to be here this soon.

I've done some hills, before the war like, but these mountains, I tell you, I loved them. It's like the harder the road gets, the faster I go. Who knew! My legs were screaming on the flat bit to the foothills and then boom – what do you know – Noré the Shark is ramming his toes into his Christophes and pedalling like a mad man. Furious!

Here comes Mercier, if he can make it through. He's a bit bulky – likes his pies – so he's having a hard time of it. I pull him through with my hand. Squeeeeeeze… Pop! Here he is.

"Are you happy, dear boy? Are you happy?" he yells. You don't have to yell, Mercier.

"What do you think?" I yell back, just as loud. He realises.

I think he's looking for me to carry on. I'm not used to this, man! Give me a chance.

"I've just won one of the hardest stages of the Tour, in front of God and in front of all these lovely people, and in front of all my competitors who I notice still haven't finished. It's amazing!"

Did I just mention God? My mum will love that.

"If I can do it in the Alps as well, I'll be doing really well. After the hell I had in Sables-Bayonne, I've got plenty to be thankful for… and my mates in Paris will love this!"

The crowd is moving, and so is Mercier, but we're going in opposite directions. Wait – I wanted to tell you about the eagles. Have you ever seen birds like that Mercier? You don't get birds like that in Paris. He's swallowed up by a mass of fuzzy suits and fuzzy faces. I'll tell him next time. The next time there's a mountain.

Stage 6

1	Honoré Barthélémy (FRA)	15h 41' 51"
2	Firmin Lambot (BEL)	+ 18' 37"
3	Jean Alavoine (FRA)	+ 33' 37"
4	Luigi Lucotti (ITA)	+ 36' 40"
5	Eugène Christophe (FRA)	+ 38' 03"
6	Léon Scieur (BEL)	+ 38' 08"
7	Jules Masselis (BEL)	+ 47' 35"
8	Émile Masson (BEL)	+ 51' 26"
9	Louis Mottiat (BEL)	+ 1h 28' 41"
10	Paul Duboc (FRA)	+ 1h 44' 24"

General Classification

1	Eugène Christophe (FRA)	
2	Émile Masson (BEL)	+ 29' 14"
3	Firmin Lambot (BEL)	+ 30' 23"

STAGE 7
LUCHON TO PERPIGNAN

Jean Alavoine

You may or may not be familiar with the mores and methods of the Tour pre-war. The 'dirty days' we call them now. Well, old Henri Desgrange, he spits every time you mention 1904. Riders leaping on trains, hanging on to cars, getting in to cars… ah, it was great to hear those stories back in the day.

But they were athletes! Real strong men like Terront and Garin, Aucouturier, Cornet. Just athletes who thought – fuck this! You want me to ride like a performing monkey? I'll show you monkey business.

I'm thinking of those boys as we hit the Col de Port. What would they have done about this? Hm? The gradients reach 15%, and OK – it's hardly the last kilometer of the Puymaurens – but I'm not riding this. Get me a taxi!

So us 'clean boys', we try not to walk, at least when

Henri is in the car behind you. And we're not even allowed to use derailleurs, which would have come in very handy today. Desgrange, being Desgrange, says they're for women and cyclo-tourists, a distinction he makes for the papers because I don't think he sees any difference between cyclo-tourists and women. "Weak and lily-livered", he would probably say.

So I walked. A couple of other lads joined in, we had a good old chinwag, so I was not alone in this rather womanly act (a Desgrangism for you there). And on the way down the Portet, what fun – I'm joined by Firmin and none other than our plucky little B-licence holder, Jules Nempon. Old last place himself, slowly being brought into the fold by Henri Desgrange who loves a story (and by trade, he ought to, I concede).

Nempon is a northern boy, not a lot unlike yours truly, although I try to hide it. I'm from Roubaix, truth be known, not Paris. Let's just keep that between ourselves.

Nempon, though - he wears it on his sleeve. Underneath that flat cap, you have a mop of unruly hair, and the wistful, doe eyes of a man who could have spent his best years down the mine. A real look of sadness about the boy, sort of disheveled and apologetic, because instead of spending his best years down a mine, he's out here enjoying himself on his bike, earning pots of money. He's riding on his own account, too, so he's busting a gut to get bonuses wherever he can, but as one of the only B-license riders left, he's getting so many bonuses, he probably gets one every time he breaks wind.

Sometimes I wonder if I shouldn't have gone solo myself, made some more money.

He's got no style, but he's a climber OK, and a good one at that. Mind you, if you were an amateur rider from Calais and you knew there's a tonne of money, a hot meal and a free soigneur laid on by the newspaper for you, you'd fly up mountains, too.

This is getting tougher. What gradient is this? I don't remember this bit in the preview...

I'm not having this. Spirit of 1904 and all that...

I pull back a little, alongside Desmarets in the Brasier. I grab onto the side of the car and get a little pull and just to distract young Bob, initiate a little conversation.

"Bob, dear boy, tell me – that rule number 35b – remind me, which one was that?"

"Ah Jean-lad, good to hear a rider interested in the intricacies of the regulations. Let me just look it up for you."

He thumbs through his rule book, and I nod at Desgrange in the back, who knows full well what I'm up to.

"Ah, Jean – there's no 35b, perhaps you were after 33c? No rider should assist any other rider or offer any support, including relaying? That one?"

"No, that's not the one I was thinking of – what's rule 32 – perhaps that was the one?"

Desgrange chuckles. Bob turns back to his book. This is the easiest ride up a mountain I've ever had. What was that about a 15% gradient?

"Don't worry, Bob, I'll catch up when I'm back at the hotel."

I'm back with Lambot and Nempon, cresting the Col de Port and they're staring wild-eyed into the distance, ghosts on the road, panting wildly. Nempon is bent double over his handlebars, the sweat lashing off him underneath his cap, his goggles steamed up.

"Nempon, you amateur, goggles off," I scream. And I can't help laughing out loud, a raw, raucous laugh. This race is crazy.

The drop is death defying. I lead them down, and by the third hairpin I see Christophe further up the mountain, the veteran bombing it down the goat paths. He'll be with us in no time, I reckon. The old man, he cometh.

Nempon and Lambot are a hairpin back, but there's no point in racing here – the Puymaurens is looming up at us like the grim reaper at the bedside. It's time to switch the back wheel round, and make the ascent up to the next checkpoint. The other guys do the same, which is a bit of light relief.

"Christ's sake, Jean-lad," pants Lambot. "You trying to run us into the ground?"

"Did you enjoy that Dejo?" I beam. I guess the answer is no.

Christophe pulls up alongside and immediately starts switching his back wheel. "Morning fellas, lovely day for a climb huh?"

Nempon is still too shy to join in, so I slap him on the back. "Ready for the Puymaurens, Pon-Pon? Look at that beast. Bet you 5f I'll beat you to the checkpoint."

"Leave him alone Jean-lad", laughs Christophe. "He'll get 20f for finishing behind you anyway."

True.

The wheel's done, but there's no point attacking them here so I wait up for the others and have a drink – better to get some water on board before the climb. I see Lambot out of the corner of my eye shaking his head at me, his mouth full of cheese sandwich.

Judgmental and a face-stuffer.

"What you got left in that musette, Dejo? Anything for me?"

He opens it and has a look inside. "Erm, I've got four more jam sandwiches, two butter sandwiches, six bananas, a bag full of figs, some chocolate... so, err... no. Nothing for you."

Christophe, who's having a piss against the wall, guffaws. "Forget it, Jean-lad, Firmin doesn't share, remember?"

"Oh go on Dejo, you can spare a sandwich – or a fig. Just a fig, come on. If I beat you up to Ax, give us a fig."

He's back on his bike, and I'm not getting a fig.

We take it easy up the bottom of the Puymaurens. This is the big climb of the day, there's no point sweating it. We've got 40km up to the top of this beast, and that could be as much as 4 hours for some of us, especially if you include the walking. The roads start to narrow quickly, and the gravel and dust is kicking up into our faces. I shift my goggles down onto my eyes, but nothing can stop the dust going into your mouth. I try wrapping my upper lip over my bottom lip, which allows me to breathe and minimises dust intake, but you try doing that while riding uphill at 20km/h.

I pull back to have a chat with Christophe.

"Hey, Eugène, what's it like being race leader eh?"

He looks at me, and gives me that 'what the fuck are you doing with your lips' look that I usually get from other riders before they try it themselves. Then he shrugs. "It's not all it's cracked up to be."

I think about this for a minute. "Bullshit."

"No, really – I'm a marked man. We're not even halfway, and the whole country thinks I'm going to win this race. Desgrange portrays me as some kind of saviour. If I get to Paris, I'll be a lucky man."

"Seen the witch lately?"

He tells me to fuck off.

Honoré Barthélémy

Today I'm riding with Mr Alavoine, he proper cracks me up he does, I like Mr Alavoine. He's one of the older guys on the Tour, and he looks it, all wrinkly in his face like your favourite cheeky uncle, the one who always gives you chocolate when your parents aren't looking. He's a big guy though, Mr Alavoine, a tough-looking guy when he wants to be, and he's gritting his teeth right now, trying to keep up with me.

And it's not like I'm the youngest guy on a bike either, I'm just young compared to this lot. I don't want to play with him, but I do keep getting away, and then I hold back because this is Mr Alavoine and he'll get you on the descent anyway, so better to have him close by I think.

I look back and we've got Mr Christophe and Mr Lambot riding together a little further away, they're doing all they can to keep up and it's showing on their faces. Mr Lambot, he's a nice man, doesn't say much, and there's some days when he doesn't say anything, looks like he's in a right mood, so he does. But when he does say something, it's usually really friendly, and he gave me a pat on the back a couple of nights ago for winning that stage, said I need to sort my flat stages out and I was proud as punch, so I was, because I knew that, but he's a great climber, one of the best.

Mr Christophe, he keeps saying I should call him Eugène, and maybe one day I will, he's leading the race now and I really want him to win, but I can't stay at his pace, I can't hang around helping people who want to draught me, I've got to go at my own pace.

Which is faster than these guys.

Sorry, Mr Alavoine, I can't wait any longer. Whoosh – what was that? That was Honoré Barthélémy, mate, the boy who can only climb. Will I see him again? Not likely.

I look back and Mr Alavoine is getting smaller in the distance, I hear him swearing, which means he's run out of jokes and he's run out of steam. The other two are struggling too, and I just keep on going, I keep on riding, I keep on clambering up this massive gradient, bump over stones, bump into other stones, it's like riding cyclocross this stage, and bump again, a jerk to the other side. This is fun, this is riding as it's meant to be.

I suck in what air is left; I'll keep it for the top which isn't far away now. Except this mountain gives you top after top, plateau after plateau, and then it lifts again and I'm like a rider in negative. I love going up when others love going down. I get faster, but then the gradient eases and I get slower. I'm a mystery to myself, man, a mystery unto my bloody self.

Here we are, then, the end of the climbs, the end of the Pyrenees, and it's downhill from here, the guys will catch me sure enough, and pfffffft there's that sound again, followed by a judder, it's the front wheel this time, just as I'm cresting the top of the Col de la Perche, I know it's the Col de la Perche because there's a sign saying well done for climbing the Col de la Perche, and sure enough, I've punctured. Well, as if they needed any more help on the descent...

I'm yanking off the tyre and throwing it away as a memento for someone, there's a young man with his bike, he's onto it like a flash. Enjoy it, fella. The pump – where's my pump? Ah man, it's not in the bag. I'm rustling around, but I can't find it anywhere. What did I do with my pump?

"Mate, you got a pump?" I shout out to the cyclo-tourist boy. "I've lost mine."

Ah shit, man, what am I going to do? Here's Mr Alavoine

and Mr Christophe, screeching to slow down to have a look as they ride past.

"Bad luck, Noré," shouts Mr Christophe. "We'll see you at the hotel."

Ah man. Don't help other riders, shouts Mr Alavoine. He waves as he rides away. Funny man when you're in the mood. Not so funny when you're not.

But a tourist can help me, yes? That's not in the rule book. The boy doesn't have one, but he's gone asking around. And look at me, standing around like a wally, does anyone have a pump at the top of this mountain?

Ah bless him, he's running back down the slope, he's got one. "Ah you beauty," I shout, and shake his hand. He's beaming and everything, I must have made his day.

"You from round here, lad?" I ask while I'm pumping this wheel up furiously.

He just looks at me, like, what did you just say Mister?

"I said are you from round these parts, young man?" because phrasing things differently to people who speak a different language is obviously the way to help him understand.

Either he's a rabbit in headlights or he really does speak another language. Funny that, eh, you hop on a bike and a few hours later, nobody understands you. I chuck him the pump, and rustle around in my musette.

"Here, lad, have a rice cake. Proper official rice cake of the Tour de France," I say ruffling the ruffian's hair. "Just don't tell Machurey."

I pop the wheel on, hop back on the bike, and wave to the lad, because waving is international isn't it? Unless waving in the Pyrenees means "watch out there's a bear behind you."

Which there isn't. Here we go, then. Descending. I have

absolutely no idea how to do this. My handlebars shake and rattle, I brake like a mad man, almost to a stop, then I pedal as hard as I can, and then brake. Stop. Round a hairpin. Then boom, fast as I can. Then brake. Stop. Wheel myself round. Ah this isn't how the other guys do it, but it's not my thing, man, just not my thing. And when I'm not climbing, the foot starts to hurt, really hurt, and I think of the boy at the top and I think – hey, there's no villages around here, none that I could see anyway, so he's had to climb here as well, isn't that great? That young lad, wherever he's from, he'd have had to climb this mountain this morning, he's been waiting all day to see us, and he gets a rice cake for finding me a pump.

Concentrate, Noré, concentrate. This is lethal, man, all the way down it is now, I memorised the route in me head last night, this is it – nothing but a descent, and I can sometimes see down the mountain, when the bushes allow it, and the other guys are miles away.

I dream of Perpignan, and the hotel. I dream of a hotel bed with cotton sheets. And I dream of living here in the mountains, with a girl and some goats, and my bike, and we'll go see that lad with the pump and we'll bring him some bread and the sun will shine and I'll take him for a ride afterwards to say I'm eternally grateful.

Henri Desgrange

Dear Reader, as you will no doubt be aware, we are halfway through this fair Tour de France, and we are short of some 60 riders, perhaps more. One loses count. However, do not allow this shortage of competitors to imply that there is a shortage of competition. For competition there is, and competition there shall be!

Am I being too upbeat? No, this is precisely what the situation requires. Upbeat, and optimistic.

Let's start that again. The start of a piece is often what makes it.

Dear Reader, how frequently I marvel at the efforts and the passion of our riders in this thirteenth Tour de France.

Yes, that's a better start.

Who would have imagined that after the difficulties involved in organising this Tour, after the number of defections from the first stage (yes, defections is a much better word, it implies a lack of courage) that we would even reach the Pyrenees, yet we find ourselves today in Perpignan, in very much the same state as it was pre-war, with a Tour that is very much 'up for grabs' as they would say in the vernacular.

I'll leave out the vernacular part. That's just for me.

We have two Frenchmen, first and fourth, and in between, two Belgians, second and third. Eugène Christophe is our leader, with three men chasing him down with immense tenacity.

Who would have imagined that our men, who travelled at such a snail's pace to Bayonne, would conquer the Pyrenean mountains, and regain their pre-war form?

Now, I have often heard of this theory that, in order that a rider should compete in a one-month Tour, he should arrive at the start line in Paris without sufficient form and mileage in the legs, and he should over time regain that form so that, by the end of the Tour, he is the victor.

This theory lacks pure common sense. The list of Tour winners is already twelve strong, and offers not one single example of a victor who sprung from nowhere in the middle of the Tour to beat his rivals either in Dunkirk or at the Velodrome itself.

Without exception, the winner has been at the peak of his powers from the very first stage, and has always been prominent in the first stages. Look at Lapize, Faber, Garrigou and Thys! From the very start of their Tour victories, they have been in peak condition.

Hmm. Thys. I accept that his Tour victories were hard-won, yet this man – this cold, money-grabbing, hard-headed shell of a man, he frustrates me so. If Thys were half the man he claimed to be, he would have accepted the hardships that this Tour were to bring, and he wouldn't have faked his illness in the first stage, for we all know that this illness was no true illness, but a cover for his frustration at not receiving the same cash payments as pre-war. If only the dunder-headed fool had stuck around, he would have been awash with money, as our fifteen men are scooping up bonuses in every town, village and hovel they pass through.

However, dear reader, we shall skip over this, and I shall not submit this in my piece for l'Auto in the morning, fear not.

Onwards. Where was I?

Ah yes, you would also be wrong to assume that it is not possible to maintain your form for the entire duration of the Tour. This musculatory effort, this month of hard labour, can only be achieved by the most highly trained of giants, our heroes, who have worked to achieve this peak condition over the winter and the spring in order to compete.

I would add that this year, the spectacle has actually been enhanced by the lack of form that our riders have brought into the competition.

Ah well, dear reader, you may have noticed that Henri Pélissier, the great shirker himself, brought into the Tour the most immense form gained from his victory in Paris-

Roubaix, and a form that he took into that particular race thanks to his participation in a large number of velodrome races. It is true that every rider suffered due to the war, there isn't a single person in this country that hasn't been affected, right down to the hermit living off the Atlantic coast on a rock. Pélissier even lost one of his brothers, but found a way – and boy, he always finds a way – to avoid the fight. "Didn't have the constitution" apparently. And those brave men I mentioned earlier, our Tour winners? Lapize, Faber... they were worth a hundred Pélissiers. I remain disgusted.

Perhaps a paragraph I shall keep to myself, dear reader.

I shall give Thys his due now. Through gritted teeth, but he does have his admirers.

Who can forget the incredible prudence taken by Philippe Thys in his two Tour victories before the war? Not only did he arrive at the start line fresh as a daisy and raring to go, but twice – for the whole month – he left nothing to chance, calculating every single move, never feeling the need to win a stage unnecessarily.

A more recent example for you. Alavoine. Look at the weight he carried with him at the start line, forcing him on the first stage to take a nap 50km from the end of the stage! But in Le Havre, the boy was in the sprint for the finish. Fourth in Cherbourg, third in Brest, and then three stage victories, including today in Perpignan. And to think that Alavoine could have been second in this Tour, just twenty minutes behind Christophe, had he not slept in that ditch and wasted his time. What pomposity!

I must also point out that form and tactics are intrinsically linked. Think of Lucotti and his foolishness on the Aubisque, wearing himself out. And why are the likes of Goethals, Nempon and Verstraeten riding high one day, and tailing off the back of the peloton the next?

They are never both out of form and tactically poor.

And if I may end with that tough old nut Duboc, whose form is gradually coming back after an awful, awful start to the Tour. It pleases me to see, in this Tour of all tours, a man like Duboc find his feet, despite the heckling of his compatriots. Why, one lackey commented that Duboc is in fine form – but only when going downhill.

Oh dear reader, what kind of Tour do we have left?

I nudge Cazenave. He's asleep.

Lucien Cazenave, you'd have a song for this, old boy. What are we to do? Fifteen riders, no more, no less. And we're halfway through the most wretched, difficult Tour of them all. Every day is a battle to acquire sufficient numbers of tyres for the boys, although with just 15 riders to supply, this task is made a little easier. Machurey has relaxed somewhat with a mere fifteen riders to provide for, and appears to pine for a return to the South-West, for what reason I do not know, but he has that longing look in his eyes and a spring in his step that I haven't seen since Nice 1913. Perhaps it's the food.

But dear reader, do we have competition? Do we have a story to write? I fear that Christophe has the Tour already in his grasp and that the Belgian Lambot is a shadow of the man who conquered the mountains in 1914. And yet, Lambot is in second place, so what chance does this give us of a spectacular Tour? Can Lambot sprint? No. Can Lambot hang on to the coattails of Christophe? Perhaps, but is this a story? Is this going to provide us with the Tour we had dreamed of?

Or do we dedicate ourselves to the efforts of our young heroes, Barthélémy, Lucotti and the like? Do we focus on the scrap for second place? Or do we try to convince you that this Tour is not all over? And that some of our riders will make it back to Paris, and that there is competition ahead; those 30 minutes Christophe has to his advantage can be frittered away with punctures and injuries?

The lights are going out in Perpignan. Finally. A light breeze outside flutters the curtains. The band has played its last downstairs, the rowdiness is petering out... the edge has finally been taken off the searing heat of the day and I shall sleep soon.

But dear reader, do I despair too soon? Am I right to doubt?

Cazenave is snoring. I should do the same.

Stage 7

1	Jean Alavoine (FRA)	13h 12' 43"
2	Eugène Christophe (FRA)	s.t.
3	Firmin Lambot (BEL)	s.t.
4	Honoré Barthélémy (FRA)	+ 10' 13"
5	Émile Masson (BEL)	+ 24' 35"
6	Léon Scieur (BEL)	s.t.
7	Paul Duboc (FRA)	s.t.
8	Jules Nempon (FRA)	s.t.
9	Jules Masselis (BEL)	+ 1h 21' 02"
10	Jacques Coomans (BEL)	+ 1h 21' 03"

General Classification

1	Eugène Christophe (FRA)	
2	Firmin Lambot (BEL)	+ 30' 23"
3	Jean Alavoine (FRA)	+ 47' 34"

STAGE 8:
PERPIGNAN TO MARSEILLE

Jean Alavoine

Ten years. Ten years since I won my first stage.

The mirror in this bathroom is cracked, but you can make out the lines on my face, sure enough. When did I get so old? So wrinkled?

Perhaps it's the sunlight. The sun has an effect on the skin, so they say. I open my mouth wide, shift it downwards, like a cow chewing grass. From one side to the other. Less wrinkly.

But the mouth pings back, and the creases reappear. Ten years.

I should have twenty stages by now. That would have just been two a year, absolutely possible even with a fit Pélissier, a Girardengo or two popping up every now and then, if he could be bothered. Share the spoils.

I should be the man who won more stages than anyone in history, not by a small margin, but by a distance. And look at me now. Ten years on, and everyone around me has either died or grown old.

Henri, my brother, he was there ten years ago. 1909, his

first Tour, we had fun. It was years before the madness started; in hindsight everything looks ridiculous. The laughter, the pushing each other around, the pillow fights. You feel guilty for having smiled.

Henri, if you could see me now – no, really – my face. I look like Dad. The bags under the eyes, the creases around the mouth… I've even started to sound like him. I can still ride a bike, Henri. I've lost the explosion of pace, but I've still got it, you'd be glad to hear. The speed is still there, it just takes a few more revolutions of the pedals to happen. I can still sprint.

I wiggle my ears. It just makes the creases worse. Is it me or are those ears getting bigger?

Henri made it halfway through the war. Fought in Belgium, then in the battle of the Marne, and then he stupidly asked to join the air force. Shot down in Pau, of all places. Pau. I shudder every time I pass through.

Henri, would you have looked like this? I squint, my eye appearing on both sides of a crack in the mirror. That's the thing, Henri, you got shot down, you never got to age. Never had to go through this. Never had to look like this.

I return to my bed. Looking too long at this face, it can get you down.

Everyone's gone, and this face wears it for them. Henri, Octave, Lucien, you'd be laughing at me if you could see me. I wonder if I would have looked like this if the war hadn't taken place. If those four years had just been four years of peace, riding bikes in the countryside like before, climbing mountains, having jokes, having a drink, pissing in the wind. Laughing.

I think of Christophe, he's older than me and he lost his brother too. Suffered as much as anyone out there, didn't ride a bike for four years. But he's not half as wrinkly as me. It's in his eyes, that's how you know. Skin's as smooth as a baby's bottom, but his eyes bear the hallmark of a man who's lived out his worst nightmares. Or Lambot, all innocent looking until you look deep into those lost eyes of his and you see what could have been.

It's all in the eyes.

I need to check again. I spring up, go back to the mirror, half hoping that I'd have changed, that it was the mirror's fault.

Those eyes. Staring back at me. Who let these eyes get so old?

Henri Desgrange

Desmarets is rifling through the checkpoint papers which are spread out on the back seat of the Brasier. It's dawn already, and we have a problem. One of our B-licence riders, a young chap by the name of Verstraeten, has been anonymously accused of cheating.

"So he signed on at every checkpoint, sir. Every checkpoint."

"You're double sure, Bob. Absolutely double sure?"

He sniffs. "Yeah, unless he asked someone to sign for him. This signature looks a little different from the rest."

It looks exactly the same. "But he arrived in Cherbourg at the precise moment the 23:20 train arrived – it is still theoretically possible that he got off the train, rode the last few hundred metres and signed at the finish line."

Bob considers this for a minute. "That means – if the train arrived spot on – then he would have had 45 seconds to get off the train, mount his bicycle, and ride."

A train has not arrived on time in this country since the Germans had their say. I very much doubt that he managed to even buy a ticket, the boy has been paying his own way in the Tour, I fail to see that this would benefit him in any way whatsoever.

"So probably not, then. Well, then, Bob – I think all the evidence points to Verstraeten not taking the train, then. Add to that the Buysse brothers claiming to have seen him struggling past when they abandoned the race, and I think we're safe to say the boy's cleared of all accusations."

Cazalis, who is driving today, leans over. He is less sure. "Fucking Belgian tried to hitch a ride holding onto my car on stage 3, remember that Henri? Remember that fucking Belgian, he thought he was being all shifty and then I wound the window down, you remember the look on his face? Remember that?"

"Indeed I do, Lucien, and please – less of the anti-Belgian rhetoric, even among friends."

He returns his eyes to the road, mindful I suppose that he is usually a much more refined man.

Perhaps a little background may be useful. Alois Verstraeten is our leading B-licence rider. B-licence, for the purposes of our discussion here being those who have opted to ride the tour as an amateur and to pay their own way. In fact, he has been rather a leading light so far in this race, at least among the aforementioned amateurs. An accusation, however, reached us by a furtively scribbled note that the Belgian rider had taken the train at some point in stage 2 between Le Havre and Cherbourg. Now, I have many reasons to doubt this, not least because all of the soigneurs were on that particular train, and not a single one of them claims to have seen him. What's more, the presence of a muddied, grey-shirted Tour de France rider on the late evening train into Cherbourg would have set tongues a-wagging, I am quite sure, and did any tongues a-wag at the time? Not a single one, which leaves me pondering why it took over a week for the news to reach us, and at Luchon of all places.

Furthermore, why didn't the accuser speak up? Why leave an anonymous note? There are rumours among the peloton that it was Dejonghe who wrote the mysterious note, but what would he have had to gain?

No, Verstraeten did not cheat, he did not take the train; in fact he could not have taken the train – a logistical impossibility, if you will. And what's more, it's 1919, not 1904 – the year of the cheat. Today's riders are athletes, not crooks and chancers. A true athlete seeks every opportunity to demonstrate his talent and push beyond his limits. You may have found Garin with his feet up in the carriage, but it simply cannot happen in the modern Tour with our more rigorous controls and our more ethical selection of riders.

"Lucien, slow down a little, I'd like to admire the scenery."

Lucien does as he's told and even entertains us with a song, perhaps one that he wrote himself, as I've never heard it before. If you've never seen this coastline, perhaps you ought to. The fresh tang of salt wafts through the open window, the sun plays lightly on the ripples in the sea. I sometimes wonder why we don't stage an entire Tour de France down here.

"Sir," Bob pipes up, "if Verstraeten didn't take the train… why is everyone saying he did?"

"Alas, Bob, if I knew… the Belgian press are furious, you know. They think we're mistreating old Alois, if only they knew how well we're treating his compatriots on the A-licences, what chances we're giving them of…"

I break off, because Lucien is screaming out of his window.

"You fucking Belgian cheat, you fuck, you! I saw that!"

"Lucien, please – a little decorum. Please tell me, what

on earth are you screaming for?"

"Your Belgian lad you were talking about, Verstrooten or whatsisface, he's been hitching a ride on that motorbike there."

I lean out and catch a sheepish looking Verstraeten peeling off the back of the motorbike.

"Tell me Lucien, what precisely did you see?"

"He had his hand on the back of that fucking motorbike, he did, proper getting a tow, the little shit."

I lean back out and we slow down to pull alongside Verstraeten.

"I say, young man – is this true? Is it true that you've been hitching a ride? You do know that means expulsion from the Tour, don't you?"

He looks at me blankly and gives a shrug. What Belgian doesn't speak French? How on earth has he been getting by these last days? And on our Fete Nationale as well, he could at least have made an effort.

"Listen, boy. You… hand… back of motorbike… cheating?"

Again, nothing from Verstraeten.

"Lucien – get to the next checkpoint, this boy's going home. Bob, sort the paperwork out, will you? Verstraeten… disqualified from the Tour, you know what to write, I presume?"

"Oh yes, sir. Looking forward to it."

And dear reader, if you think I enjoy this, if you think I derive any pleasure whatsoever from the expulsion of a rider, then you are wholly mistaken. I catch your glances every now and then, I know you believe me to be an unduly harsh man, and heaven knows, I must play this role to its fullest, but it pains me to see a man – a man – who has wasted his opportunities in life. We have given Alois Verstraeten every chance to prove his worth, and he has, until this very moment, taken those opportunities with both hands. For a B-licence rider to reach this stage of the most arduous of Tours is an achievement, I gladly applaud the boy.

But if a Tour is tough, if a Tour is a struggle, it is designed to be so, in order that the very best of men prove themselves to be the very, very best of men. And that the wastrels by the side of the road, with their Auto folded up in their back pocket, look upon these men and say to themselves "I must do better, I must be more like them", well this is precisely the objective of the Tour. It is not to enjoy oneself, it is to be an example. A good example. Were I to broaden our horizons, the objective of the Tour is not for one man to win the race, nor is it for the sport of cycling to win the hearts and minds of the public. The objective of the Tour is to improve men. Therefore, it must be tough. It must be fair. The Tour must set the example.

Alois Verstraeten, dear reader, is a bad example. A rotten example. And cry as he might, plead as no doubt he will at the next checkpoint, he is going back to Belgium on the next available train, and he's paying for it himself.

Jean Alavoine

Here's a slow-moving train of aches and pains on its way out of Perpignan. Masselis, one of the Belgians, is grunting and moaning with every pedal stroke. Lambot is complaining about the heat; he says it's going to melt his cheese sandwiches. Masson's banging on about his knee.

And Eugène is in a sulk. When Eugène's in a sulk, it's like you're all obliged to be in an equally bad sulk.

It's heavy going, too. A muggy, sodden sort of summer night, the type where people are lying in bed right now – which is where I should be – sweating and complaining about the oppressive heat. That kind of no-blanket, no-duvet night. And here we are, by moonlight, riding the coastline in search of a breeze or some kind of relief.

I'm in no mood to socialise today. I feel old. And crabby.

Here's Steux, another Belgian.

"Jean-boy, got a ciggie?"

"I'm rationing them today, lad."

"Ah come on, I'm gasping here, give us one."

I give in, just to ride in a little silence for a while.

He grasps at it, rams it in his wretched little mouth and fumbles around for a light. Yes, I have one. For Christ's sake.

He takes one drag.

"You know, when I was riding the Tour of Belgium back in 19...."

Oh fuck this. I'm off.

"Oi, Desgrange," I shout through the window of his pimp-mobile. "I'm going bonus-hunting. Better than sticking around with this slow-moving misery-train."

Here's one good thing about this Tour. Now there's only a handful of us left, there's bonuses a-plenty if you want them. Wherever you go, there's a local café or a greengrocer offering a couple of francs to the first rider through town, or the last rider to a checkpoint. There's a mechanic in Peyriac who's offering 3f for the third rider past his garage, of all things.

And this is on top of the bog-standard bonuses you get. Everywhere you go, they're chucking money at you.

Old Henri, he comes round the day later with all the bonus money, and half the time you had no idea there was 2 francs for coming last at a checkpoint, or 5 francs for the first Frenchman in town.

Some riders aren't that bothered about the bonuses. Lambot lolls around at the back of the peloton half the time, or hangs off the shoulder of Christophe, letting Eugène take the bonus or what's left of the bonuses. He's got his eyes on a bigger prize, I imagine. But he's missing out.

And then there's the completely random bonuses that just seem to get made up on the spur of the moment. I was given 50 francs by someone nobody had ever heard of for coming through first at the top of a hill so insignificant I didn't even notice it. 50 francs for climbing a molehill.

So frankly, who wants to piss around in a moaning, groaning peloton when you can chase down a bit of wonga?

I've got a tail, though.

I have a second or two to glance round. Squat. Flat cap. Ugly action. Oh no, it's Duboc. Oh that's all I need. And he's brought a Belgian with him. Masselis. Fucking wonderful.

What greater incentive do you need than having to spend the afternoon with Apple-Boy and a non-entity from the middle of nowhere. Let's step on it.

Duboc's screaming at me from down the road.

"Wait up – we can share out the bonus money Jean-boy!"

Share? Did he actually say share? Do one, Apple-boy. I crush the pedals again, but they're closing in on me. Actually relaying. Masselis seems to have regained a bit of form, too.

"Piss off will you? Can't you see I want to be on my own?"

Duboc spits. He doesn't seem to care.

"There's 5 francs for the first man through Narbonne, you know," he grins that toothy grin at me, as if I didn't know – as if it were some secret he's just found out.

"Of course I bloody know, you fool."

And with a final sprint, I shake them off and welcome the people of Narbonne to my world. Look at them. They actually woke up to see me. 5 francs for me. Ker-ching.

The big money comes later. We have 20 francs in Nimes, 15 in Aix – and that's just one of the prizes. There's another 40 francs on offer from an arts school for the first man through the town. Nempon, as always, will be on the lookout for the prize money for the last man through town – if he's interested, there's 10 francs for the last man into Marseille.

Duboc and Masselis are back on my tail. What an interesting pair they make. Duboc is that classless type of rider from way before the war. Time was he could have blossomed into an athlete, but he went the other way. A bulldog on a bike, stinking of fermented fruit. He's the kind of rider who would always ride in a brown woollen suit if he could, but convention now dictates he has to wear 'sports clothes', and he hates it.

Masselis is a danger, though. I remember he won a stage a couple of years before the war. He looks like a modern rider, all limbs and clean shaven, and he's got a decent turn of pace. I should watch out for him in Beziers.

"Let us have a turn, Jean-boy," Duboc hollers from behind.

"Yeah, I need to pay for some repairs tonight," shouts Masselis. And I almost feel sorry for him.

Almost. Before I shower them with dust from my back wheel.

Eugène Christophe

There's a noise and a smell that hit you whe[n]
reach Marseille. Neither is pleasant. And it has t[o]
strong odour to overpower the smell of our mini pe[
Lambot hasn't left my side all day, and he stinks o[
own piss which is worrying for both of us. Goethal[s]
been smoking his rotten cigarettes almost non-stop,
Duboc just smells of Duboc.

But the noise. It's not the same noise that you hea[r]
Brest or Perpignan. The people of Marseille, the gr[
unwashed plague of swarthy, angry southerners, th[
make a noise several semitones below that of other fini[
towns.

We slow instinctively. Alavoine thinks we're playing, bu[t]
we're afraid.

Scieur, the Belgian, leans over.

"Is it as bad as they say?"

"Worse," I reply. "A hundred times worse."

"Is it safe?"

"I bloody hope so, Léon."

The third thing you notice on entering Marseille – after
the noise and the smell – is the brightness. The buildings
are a beige-white and the sky is a darker blue. The roads
are as unkempt as anywhere in the country, not through
war – although they'd have gladly welcomed the fighting,
but because nobody in Marseille cares about Marseille.

And that's what makes it so dangerous.

That noise is growing to a crescendo. Word has got
around. Or we're getting closer. Or both.

Goethals has dropped off the back, the effort of smoking
twenty cigarettes over 300 kilometres has obviously taken
its toll on him. He'll have to face them alone.

2km to go, according to a handmade sign, and the

crowds are starting to thicken. From one deep to two deep, to a roar to a bellow, you can only hope and pray that there's a way from the finish line to safety, or there won't be 15 riders at the start line when we leave this place.

"What do you reckon's going to happen Cri-Cri?" shouts Jean-boy.

"Fists, at best. Weapons at worst."

"Fucking hell. We should have stopped at Aix."

"You're still going to sprint for the stage though aren't you?" I wink.

He nods. Of course he will.

Jean picks up the pace, so I follow. I bend over the handlebars to keep up with him, straining the effort. Suddenly the crowd start to blur, this is fast. Lambot, of course, is straight onto my tail. We've lost Duboc, I can smell it. But we've gained Lucotti, the little Italian, who is showing a new-found aggression.

A technical bit now – we have to slow right down for a left-hander, and then a sweeping right-hander allows us to pick up speed and Alavoine's off again, acceleration after acceleration, boy he's good at this.

For a split second, I think I can hang on to his wheel. Every rider has that moment of false belief, that moment where the mind transcends the body and the body responds just that instant too late – no, no we can't do this, remember your place. I remember my place and the body responds by easing off the pedals. Same for Lambot, who has seen the future too.

But the future isn't always as clear as you thought. Alavoine has won, but the barriers are down and the crowd are on him. It's not to slap his back, either. I release my feet from the pedals but stay on the bike, ramming into the crowd, shoulder-first. Jean-boy is throwing punches as race officials try to puncture their way into the seething

mass. A baseball bat smashes into my back wheel, which mercifully holds, and I slam into a man covered in scars who is about to launch another attack on Alavoine.

Lambot is joining in now, and Duboc is off his bike throwing punches too. Another man swings at me but I duck out of the path of his punch.

A gap appears in the crowd and Jean-boy is first through it – I follow and some race officials appear to have cleared a way through.

"Lads – through here," I yell, but Duboc and a couple of Belgians are slugging it out with locals.

"Oi – get out of here – NOW," I scream at him, which gets his attention. A woman falls against my bike, her blue dress getting caught in the wheel momentarily, and the crowd are in again. I manage to hold myself upright, and jump off the bike to wheel it into the café where the owners are creating a cordon for the riders to run through.

"Sorry about the local welcome," says the waiter, straining as he holds back the snarling mob. A slobber of spit lands on his shoulder.

Desgrange is inside. Jean is leaning over him.

The words 'fucking' and 'murder' are repeated several times, while old Henri looks downcast, offering excuses about the local police force, municipality, disorganised, and so on and so on. I'm not getting involved.

I need to find out where I'm staying, who I'm staying with, and how I'm going to get out of this café alive.

Stage 8

1	Jean Alavoine (FRA)	13h 50' 32"
2	Luigi Lucotti (ITA)	s.t.
3	Léon Scieur (BEL)	s.t.
4	Firmin Lambot (BEL)	s.t.
5	Eugène Christophe (FRA)	s.t.
6	Paul Duboc (FRA)	s.t.
7	Honoré Barthélémy (FRA)	+ 7' 50"
8	Joseph Van Daele (BEL)	s.t.
9	Félix Goethals (FRA)	+ 13' 33"
10	Jules Nempon (FRA)	+ 21' 04"

General Classification

1	Eugène Christophe (FRA)	
2	Firmin Lambot (BEL)	+ 30' 23"
3	Jean Alavoine (FRA)	+ 47' 34"

STAGE 9
MARSEILLE TO NICE

Henri Desgrange

Filthy. Unwashed. Dirty. Violent. Marseille, you have done yourself no favours. I thought the war would have made you see sense, your men sent to the lines, fighting in the trenches, they may have resolved to live healthier lives.

Not the men of Marseille.

And why could we not have block-booked a hotel in this God-forsaken city? One more flight of stairs in this hovel, for a few mumbled words from Vandaele and Steux, before travelling 30 minutes to the other side of town for a few mumbled words from Lambot.

We would have done better to finish in Aix. In this heat...

I knock at the door. No response. Is that snoring I hear from inside? Dear lord, they're still in bed. Belgians...

Eugène Christophe

11am

Here's a thought. At what point do you imagine winning the Tour? I imagined it in 1913, I imagined it too soon. But here, among old men, I imagine that if my bike holds – and if my body holds – I could win this Tour. My biggest rivals are those old men. Alavoine, who has filled his pockets with bonus money and has settled into a less aggressive tempo today. He's the man in form, and has been surprisingly quick over the mountains so far.

Lambot, who started this race as if he hadn't ridden a bike in five years. In fact, he probably hadn't ridden a bike in five years. But everywhere you go, there's Lambot. You think you've shaken him off, he's ten metres behind you, face like death, but boy, the Belgian has an engine.

And Scieur, the locomotive, the genial old Belgian who never stops riding. Léon punctured about a thousand times on the first two stages, and yet he keeps finding tyres, he keeps repairing his last inner tubes and stocking up the next day, he keeps riding.

These old men are breathing down my neck, each of us realising that this Tour might be our last, that our ageing bodies might at some point just give way. We let the young boys ride ahead, and we reel them in day after day, but one day they'll ride ahead and we won't find the reserves, we won't find the extra juice that powers the legs at a higher cadence. We don't have long.

Any open wounds will be taking a battering today. The Mistral is whipping into us from the left, and venture too close to the edge of the route between Frejus and Aix-en-Provence, and the scorched grass, sharpened by the dry, warm Mistral winds, will cut you to ribbons. So you ride on the camber and you hunt for a shield – a human one, if you can get it. Desgrange hates it when we ride like this, but there are boys still in this Tour who realise they can earn a few bonuses if they protect the riders who have a chance of winning.

Jules Nempon, the plucky little northern boy, he plays a coy game, but he's as sly as any other rider. Who else would be desperate to come in last? He's been my Mistral Minder for the last five kilometres, and in exchange, I'll let him ride ahead for any bonuses he's got planned. The trick is to match your front wheel to his back wheel, overlapping every so slightly. In a bigger peloton – there are just 12 of us left now – we'd create an echelon if Henri would allow it and we'd relay all the way home. I'm just happy to have one man to break the wind.

By the time we reach Nice for the first time, we're all back together. The mountain boys Lucotti and Barthélémy have been caught, but once we're back onto the Col de Braus, they'll be leaping away again, finding joy in the gradient. While they race, I have to keep my eye on the old boys.

Honoré Barthélémy

2pm

Luigi is a tricky rider, man. A tricky rider.

He's been telling me about Nice, like it's his home town (it isn't) but it's full of Italians and they'll be welcoming him like a hero, so can I let him go through Nice first and then once we hit the Sospel circuit, we can start racing, and I was thinking why not, you go ahead, man, you go ahead. And then Mr Alavoine and Mr Christophe suddenly appeared on the horizon and they were chasing us down, the old men chasing the young men, and Luigi was yelling at me to go faster and I was saying – that's your job, Luigi, that's your job. Do your work on the front.

And then we argued for a bit, and the figures in the distance got bigger and bigger until they weren't in the distance any more and they were laughing at us.

"Hello kids!" shouted Mr Alavoine, but he did it in a nice way, with that sparkle in his eye.

"Had fun today?" smirks Mr Christophe. Mr Lambot's behind him and he's looking tired, he doesn't say a thing.

I tell them I'm waiting to have my fun, and that we should let Luigi go through Nice first on his own and they agree, it's a nice idea.

So we ride easy, because the worst is yet to come on this stage, and we take in the scenery. There's the bay of Theoule, says Mr Christophe, and then some islands in the distance, I don't catch their name, and the sea is like a carpet of diamonds, it's so beautiful, you just want to touch it. A sign says Antibes, so we can't be far from Nice now, and every rider – except Luigi – is gawping at the palm trees that line the boulevards. And if you look ahead, you can see mountains – with snow on them. That's where we'll be tomorrow, says Mr Alavoine. Watching you climb, he adds.

I could ride roads like these all day, it's like you're not actually riding your bike, like you could just ease off the pedals and the road's doing all the moving for you. Beautiful.

And Nice is lovely too. A big long promenade, and there's people everywhere. Luigi's showboating now, waving at everyone. Mr Alavoine shouts ahead and tells him to get on with it, but it's proper heart-warming how the local riders get to nip ahead and soak up the love from the crowd. Even if they're not really Italians, not proper ones anyway, but they like Luigi and he seems to like them.

3pm

Mr Christophe told me I should read the course book on the rest day, he said if I knew the routes better, I'd be a more 'tactical' rider. So I studied the book all day yesterday and I'm ready for the circuit around the Sospel.

The first bit, the bit I'm on now, is where I shake off Luigi and the others. The col de Nice is short and sharp, but there's enough of it to really put some distance in. That's the plan, and it's working. I look round at Luigi, and he's trying all he can to hang on, but the older guys are taking it easy, they're not pushing on at all. It's just me and the Italian.

Next on the route map, it shows a vertical climb. I've got it in my mind now, etched like a photograph. It's called the Col de Braus, it looks straight when you see the diagrams in the paper, but when you look at the actual map, you know this is going to hurt.

And it is hurting, but thanks to Mr Christophe, I was ready for this. I know that in 100 metres, it's going to ramp up to 10% and each hairpin's going to get harder. Where's the Italian gone? Shit, he's alongside me!

"Hey Honoré, you thought you'd leave me?"

Actually, Luigi, I did.

So I put some extra gas in the engine. The crowd close in so only one man can get through at a time, and that first man is me. The Italians don't like it, but I'm pouring all I've got into this, but then the Italians are roaring like crazy and I don't know why, the pain is blacking me out.

The crowd are three deep and I can feel a rush of wind on my left hand side, and it's not just Lucotti, it's Lucotti and a train of Italians waving their flags, pushing him on and I can't hold on. There's more hairpins still to go, how many I've lost count, but it seems every pedal stroke I put in, Luigi puts in two. Man, this boy can ride.

I'm like a punctured balloon, I'm going so slowly I might as well be falling backwards. A shot of pain rips through my forehead and my eyeballs feel like they'll fall out. Ah this can't go on. This isn't even a proper mountain.

Lucotti's three hairpins ahead, soon to be four. Stay on, Noré, stay on.

I feel like heaving, a proper urge to throw up whatever Machurey had put in that baguette down there in Nice. But on we go. Up we go. Luigi's five ahead. Five!

Each hairpin is a needle rammed into my thighs, another into my eyes. I look down, you should never look down. Why did I look down? Look at the two metres in front of you, Noré, only the two metres in front, never behind, never up, never down, just focus on those two metres.

This is helping; this is the way I should have been riding all the way up. Two metres, no more. Get through these two, and the next two, and the next two. Tick them off, there'll be a dip soon into Sospel, I can catch my breath there. Forget Luigi. Forget the race. Just get to the top.

When it comes, I feel like a drowning man reaching the surface. Like a man at the bottom of the deepest ocean who swims up, higher and higher, still not reaching the surface of the water, where is it – why am I not able to breathe – and you kick up and up, until finally the water breaks and you breathe in as much air as your lungs can handle. And you stop before you drop to flip the gears and you go, leaving the pain behind you.

Sospel is a checkpoint. I sign without getting off the

bicycle, I see Luigi has a minute and a half on me. A minute and a half, man. That's not so bad.

He won't have stopped, so I don't stop either. All it takes is a puncture, or a fall, but I don't want that to happen to Luigi. Nobody wants to lose on a puncture after doing all this. That's pure wrong.

This bit, I remember. The col de Castillon, and it's sharp. I flip my back wheel first, get a climbing gear back on. More French fans here, they're giving me a push. I reach the top and hear that sound, the worst sound, the squishy feeling and the thudding and scraping. A pfffft from the front wheel.

Come on, man, not now. Dismount, swing your legs off. Done. Tyre from the shoulders, side of the road. Waiting. Rip the tyre off the wheel, easy. Toss it to the side of the road. Check. Stretch the tyre out. Quick. Whack it on, pump it up. Come on, come on. What will he be now, three minutes?

Now go. Go now go.

Back down into Menton, it's a neck-breaker this and half of me says I should look up because over there, that's Monaco and over there that's Nice, and down there, that's Menton, and over that way is Italy, and all of this I'll never see if I don't look now, but I've got this race you see, you'll all have to wait, and maybe I'll come back one day and look up, but now it's just down, down, down. Hairpin follows hairpin, rocks follow ravines. No crowds here.

Oh ho, what's this? Luigi, getting back on his bike, a few hundred metres ahead of me. What happened to you poor boy? Nobody wants to lose on a puncture.

I remember my training again. Mr Christophe, he said that when you've got a target, you reel him in like a fish. Never let him get away. Once you've got a man in your sights, you can match your pedal strokes to his. Provided you've both got the gears to match, you start to equal him. And he can't see you; he can't see you're closing in on him. So you go that tiny bit faster. I'm reeling Luigi in, taking his rhythm and speeding it up.

But oh, Luigi. Oh no, not now. Not while I'm beating you fairly. His back wheel kicks out, the tyre flapping off the wheel, it looks like it was his last one too. There's none on his shoulders. Oh Luigi. I hear your screams. Che caaaaAAAAAZZZZOOOOoooooo as I pass him. Oh Luigi.

I reeled you in, but you were already dead.

Firmin Lambot

That noise. Is it my wheel?

No, I'm fine... it's Christophe's! Instinct takes over; I can take two minutes if I hit him hard now. Suddenly I feel no pain. I feel no aches.

Christophe disappears behind me; I've got 20km to put the knife in.

Eugène Christophe

5pm

Lambot. Who else.

I don't blame him – I'd have attacked on a puncture, too. But to have had two minutes' lead on the Belgian and to have lost it on a puncture 20km from the finish, that's bad form. Firmin Lambot, the man you can never shake off, picking up the bodies as he coasts to the finish.

The tyre is on, and I leap back on my saddle. I imagine it's 500m, maybe 750 now, that Lambot has got on me. I'm on my own again – the climbers have probably finished already; it's just the old men battling it out for the places.

I was ahead of Lambot on the Sospel, and wheel to wheel with him on the col de Castillon. Jean-lad and Léon were pushing themselves to the limit but now they've both gone on ahead, and I'm the last of the leaders, losing time on everyone.

Push, Eugène, push. This isn't going to cut into Lambot's lead. We all saw the way he joined in the attack on Pélissier, and now he's cutting into me. I had nearly 30 minutes on him at the start of the day, he'll eat into every second until we get to Paris. I can't let him take any more. It sets a precedent.

Palm trees line the boulevard, there can't be long left. Perhaps all I have to hope for is that I cut Lambot's advantage. I'm no sprinter like Alavoine, I'm no climber like Barthélémy, but I can roll, and I'll roll at as high a cadence as my old body can push me. The Mistral has gone, and I can rely on a gentler, saltier sea breeze. Head down, check that new front tyre, they might not last long in this Tour but when they're fresh, and properly inflated, you feel you have an extra second or two in every kilometre, so long as it lasts.

The finish line is ahead of me, it's come quicker than I had expected. Every second counts.

And then… the finishing line disappears. Who took it away? I've lost all control of the bike, and as time slows down, I can see the ground getting closer, my leg trapped under the bike has nowhere to go, and the gravel starts cutting slowly into my skin, stone by stone. My arm is next to hit, I can see it happening, I need to protect my head so my shoulder needs to come next, but the momentum is forcing my head to the ground too quickly. I'm moving, somehow, and the ground is ripping skin from my knee. My shorts are tearing, and I can see each thread come apart as it happens.

It's the witch.

She's here, in Nice. Her green teeth sharpened, her filthy fingernails digging into my scalp. The pain hasn't started yet, but it's come with an advance warning from the witch, this is just the beginning, as the threads come apart on my clothes, my whole Tour is untangling in front of me.

Have I stopped? I appear to be still, and if I just lay here and close my eyes, perhaps it never happened and perhaps I'll heal in time, if everyone just leaves me alone.

I'm spitting grit, and there's blood – lots of blood. My right knee is fucking pouring a dark red. How did I end up down here? Play it back, Eugène, where did it go wrong?

A policeman is standing over me, saying something – is he apologising? That was it; I hit him. He hit me. Which way round is it? The witch has many ways of bringing a cyclist down – I had hoped for hunger, oh I could cope with hunger, but the blood, the pain is ratcheting up from a dull thud to a screeching wail emanating from my knee. I can't even get up.

The recall is getting sharper. I see it now. Just after the finish line, he stepped out of the crowd, straight into my path – I had nowhere to go, not a second to react. I'm picking myself up, but the knee isn't following, it's a red streaming flow of blood and it won't shift from the road. Anger contains the pain, or does pain release the anger?

"You total fucking shit", I'm spitting with rage, so it's the pain that releases the anger. I push him in the chest and there are race officials pulling me back, Cazalis with his restraining arms, all suit and hair.

"That shit cost me my Tour − look at me, look at my fucking knee. Where's Desgrange? Where's Henri? Tell him this fucking copper has just ruined my race. How does he expect me to get back to Paris like this?"

"Cri-Cri, leave it − he didn't look, he didn't see you." It sounds like Alphonse. I only see a red mist and a red leg.

I'm carried, flaying, in a circle − the policeman is getting further away without moving. Cazalis is whispering softly in my ear, but now the pain has given way to fear and worry, and the tears are flowing, if Desgrange were to see this, I'd be a sorry op-ed in the morning, I'm saying keep me away from Desgrange, keep Desgrange away from me, the pen is mightier than the policeman. If I'm finished, I want to be finished for good, not finished by the shame of a Desgrange editorial.

My soigneur has that look on his face, that look that says I've seen this before, and it's not good, but the fear and the worry are giving way to something else now, what is it? Defiance? Look at me like that, and I'll defy you all the way to Paris, I'll ride with one leg if need be, cut it off if that's what it takes, shame me in your yellow rag, if you will, look at me with pity if you want, but I'll ride off whatever it is the witch has cursed me with.

I'll ride you all to hell and back.

Léon Scieur

This has to be a joke. Where are my clothes? I'm filthy with sweat, my riding kit is soaked through, and I've searched every inch of this hotel room (again, many thanks Desgrange and co, you've excelled yourself with these one-star hotels), and my clothes are clearly not present. Absent. Missing in action.

Dejo's just come in, still in his cycling gear.

"You neither?" he gestures.

"What the hell are we meant to do?"

"I'm starving as well – there's no way I'm going to the restaurant in these clothes. I need food, Paupou."

Firmin always needs food. But we both need our clothes. I check in on the French. Alavoine is next door today, and he's laid out on his bed, wearing nothing but a bathrobe, rifling through his many letters – probably looking for more velodrome contracts.

"15 hours on the road, fellas. 15 hours, and we still got here before our clothes!" he beams. He then leaps up, tightens his bathrobe and adjusts his balls.

"Shall we dine, gentlemen?"

Firmin's the first to run in and find his bathrobe. I shrug; might as well join in.

Alavoine jumps up and dances down the hallway, knocking on doors. "Bathrobes on, gents, there's an Italian restaurant across the road and Desgrange is buying the pizza."

Laughter all round. I knock on Goethals' door, there's no answer.

"He's gone home," shouts Firmin from behind his door, "haemorrhoids."

I wince. What a way to go. You ride halfway around France, you survive the north and the west wind, you reach Nice – and you get piles. Poor fella.

"And the old fella's smashed his knee up, don't expect him to come."

Ah yes, the valiant Cri-Cri, brought a-cropper by a copper.

Barthélémy, our valiant stage winner, is limping down

the corridor in his bathrobe. "Did someone say pizza? Me nuggets are really hurtin', I hope it's not far," and the Italian boy Lucotti – who is practically in his own country here – is behind him with a bottle of cognac in hand.

"Leave that behind, lad, Henri's paying tonight. He doesn't know it yet, but he's paying."

We're joined by Duboc who looks like he's never worn a white bathrobe in his life, but this is the Tour, this is Nice, we're all entering unchartered territory now. Come on apple boy, come on lads. Let's eat.

Alavoine is leading the dance, he looks quite the part, and as we pass through the hotel lobby, heads are turning – some of the women are wolf-whistling. Jean-lad stops, and we all bunch up behind, clashing into one another. He's making a point of this.

"Ladies and gentlemen," he proclaims, looking more and more like Caesar. "We came here today to entertain you, but even the entertainment needs entertaining from time to time. Please, have a marvellous evening, and tell your friends that the Giants of the Road are wearing nothing underneath their bathrobes!"

Duboc tightens his robe further, a look of unease on his face. Poor lad. Never had to do this in the orchards.

And we're outside, in the warmth of the Mediterranean sun, and there isn't a single person in the street who isn't pointing at us or talking about us. A couple of urchins run up and ask for Lucotti's signature, he's only too happy to oblige, and of course he's brought the cognac with him.

Jean-lad leads us across the road, stopping traffic as he goes, before pushing open the restaurant doors.

"A table for the Giants of the Road, please, and make sure the tab gets passed on to Monsieur Henri Desgrange, who is residing at the hotel across the road, room 43. Red face, white moustache, you'll know him when you see him."

We're led to a round table in the middle of the restaurant, and I'm suddenly conscious of a gap opening up in my bathrobe. Quick, Léon, sit down, cover up. Hide your modesty.

"Allora, ragazzi," shouts Lucotti. "Siamo casa mia stasera!"

Now, I don't speak Italian, but I'm guessing the young Italian boy is happy to be in Nice, which is to all intents and purposes, an Italian city.

"Easy, boy," says Jean-lad. "There's a thousand eyes on you tonight, and five hundred of them will be reporters' eyes. Whatever you do will end up in the pages of l'Auto. So try to be a little less... showy."

"He's alright, Mr Alavoine," adds Barthélémy. "He's just proper excited to be home aren't you Luco?"

"The drinks are on me!" screams the Italian, oblivious to the press coverage.

The waiter brings bread, which Lambot tears into immediately.

I turn to Duboc. "So Paul, are you going to touch the food tonight? So long as Machurey's not cooking, right?"

He gives me the eye, but loosens up, at last. "That guy couldn't cook his way out of a paper bag, he's trying to kill me I know it. Kill us all, he would."

I laugh. "Oh come on Paul, you're not still worried about being poisoned are you?"

"Damn right I am. Did you try that chocolate? Revolting, it was. I swear there was arsenic in it."

Alavoine slaps him on the back. "Apple-boy, there's as much arsenic in that as there is water in Luigi's bottle of cognac over there. So, boys, we've spent the last couple of weeks whining about the Tour, but what's the best thing about this race, eh?"

Scratching heads. Fumbled silence. There must be something…

"The mountains!" shouts Honoré.

"Good shout, boy!"

"And I'm going to live at the top of a mountain with a nice girl and settle down and have children there, and I'll cycle down the hill every day and cycle back up with some bread and we'll have goats and everything. That's what I'm going to do."

Laughter all round. And why not. We're all warming to this lad.

"Sorting the Pélissiers out," adds Lambot. "That felt good."

"That nearly killed us all," I pitch in. "But the look on Henri's face when they peeled him off the floor in Sables, that was worth it. I've never ridden that fast in my life."

Alavoine leans in. "You know what, those boys, they're proper cyclists. I mean us, we're good, good enough to get this far, but those two… if only they had the balls to match their talent, they'd be world-beaters."

Barthélémy: "Is it true Henri dodged the war?"

"Yes and no, Noré, yes and no… he was drafted, and he fought, but you were more likely to find him on the velodrome than on the front. He rode in Italy, too. They said he didn't have the constitution for the fight. Lost his brother, like me, but you know what – nobody really knows what anyone else did for those four years. We can talk, we can speculate, but really, we don't know. All we know is that Henri is a splendid cyclist. He's just a bit of a twat."

"My best thing," my turn now. "The French women."

Ahhhs all round. A raise of glasses. A refill.

"Tell us more, Loco," asks Jean-lad.

"They're so… feisty. Proper women, they are. Don't you

look at them as you're riding past?"

A few nods. Obviously they do. "There was this one, somewhere near Brest, you could tell she was a proper Breton girl, hardy yet elegant, she had this auburn hair that fell to her shoulders, her fists were clenched, her breasts were heaving. You could put her to work on the farm one day and take her to the ball the next. That's what you want from a woman."

"I missed that one," says Duboc, genuinely disappointed.

The pizzas have arrived, and silence has fallen, all of us thinking about the Breton girl with the hair and the breasts. It's been two weeks and we've flogged ourselves at the altar of this Tour, at the service of Desgrange, and these are the moments we cling to. Breton girls with flowing hair and heaving breasts. Eating pizza in a bathrobe while the world looks on, bemused. The rosé wine and the tiramisu, the feeling of being just another human being in a normal world full of normal people, just for a short while, rather than the semi-mythical creatures we're supposed to be for the benefit of the newspapers. We're just men. And that feels good.

Stage 9

1	Honoré Barthélémy (FRA)	13h 39' 48"
2	Luigi Lucotti (ITA)	+ 6' 09"
3	Alfred Steux (BEL)	+ 13' 37"
4	Jean Alavoine (FRA)	+ 16' 12"
5	Léon Scieur (BEL)	s.t.
6	Firmin Lambot (BEL)	s.t.
7	Eugène Christophe (FRA)	+ 20' 12"
8	Félix Goethals (FRA)	+ 35' 52"
9	Joseph Van Daele (BEL)	+ 48' 56"
10	Paul Duboc (FRA)	+ 1h 01' 57"

General Classification

1	Eugène Christophe (FRA)	
2	Firmin Lambot (BEL)	+ 26' 23"
3	Jean Alavoine (FRA)	+ 43' 34"

STAGE 10
NICE TO GRENOBLE

Eugène Christophe

I am not a vain man. I will gladly suffer the slings and arrows of the peloton, as any rider should. I'm old enough not to care, and wise enough to realise it's because I'm one of them. But this morning's events will live with me.

It started this lunchtime with Desgrange, master of ceremonies, holding sway in the Café, with his "major announcement" about the future of the Tour. What could it be? There were rumours that Desgrange was going to resign, but he'd die sooner than give this up. Some said that he would be increasing the number of stages to 20, or making us ride as international teams next year.

But no. None of these rumours would have been grandiose enough for old Desgrange. His announcement, his "major statement" was simple enough − there was to be a new jersey so that fans could easily spot the leader of the tour. A jersey that would make the race leader 'stand out' from the peloton.

A yellow jersey.

Yellow. Yellow, the colour of cowardice, of betrayal, of a cuckold. The colour of madness. There's a perfectly good reason why people don't wear yellow, why they don't make their children wear yellow. That's because it's YELLOW.

"You are fucking joking me," I seem to remember saying. Not that Desgrange noticed, full of himself as always, he carried on, something about the "enormous challenges that face our giants of the road, the Galibier, Strasbourg, the cobblestones…" and so on and so on, as I stood there, facing the laughter and jibes of the other riders.

Alavoine: "Hey, Canary Christophe, can we take you down the mine?"

Steux: "What's your wife up to today, Cri-Cri?"

A yellow jersey. Imagine the shame.

"Go on, put it on Cri-Cri", urged the crowd. Desgrange held it aloft, a rictus grin on his red and white face, unwittingly drawing laughs from the other riders.

This is the Worst. Day. Ever.

I felt my soul depart from my body in shame as I pulled on the puke-coloured jersey. Desgrange led the applause, oblivious to the howls of derision and laughter. And I stood there, like a lemon. Quite literally.

In grey, there was a union of sorts. The professionals, all together, on one team, recognisably as one. And my punishment for riding the best Tour of my life? Humiliation.

We left Nice at 2am in pitch black darkness, with only the headlamps of Desgrange's Brasier to light the way, and the moonlight off the Mediterranean illuminating my yellow jersey. As always, we stuck together – this time for warmth as much as anything else – which gave Jean-lad even more opportunities to mock me.

"Slow down Cri-Cri, I was just reading Desgrange's

editorial on your back."

"If you hadn't slept in that ditch, you'd be wearing this abomination, Jean-lad."

He yawns, fake stretches, and says "I'll get another twenty minutes today, in that case. Who needs to win the Tour when you're rich."

The only rider who seems to want the jersey is Lambot, a little too careful not to crack any jokes about the colour yellow in case he ends up wearing it the next day. Yellow or grey, Lambot would wear a dress if it meant winning the Tour.

There are now multiple races within the race. There's the race for the overall and realistically only Firmin Lambot is threatening me. He's 30 minutes back, and is hanging around behind me every inch of the way, keeping me within his line of vision so that – if I puncture or fall – he can attack, as he has done several times already. Then there's the race for the mountains, not that you get a prize for reaching the top of the mountain first, but Honoré Barthélémy and the Italian Lucotti are fighting that one out themselves. And then there's Jean Alavoine, racing himself mostly because no one else is faster than him on the flat, and he wants two things: bonus money and velodrome contracts.

It's early morning, and the gradient has been building since we left Nice. This is Colmars, a checkpoint and Roux is in charge of this one – journalist at l'Auto and one of the good ones. I look down at the signatures, and Barthélémy put pen to paper three minutes ago. Roux gives me a pat on the shoulder and shouts 'Allez Cri-Cri' as I get back on my bike. He seems to hold onto the pen a little longer for Lambot, but as we cross the bridge and take a tight right into the old town, the Belgian is back on my tail. This guy is a limpet.

Easy now, Cri-Cri. Cat and mouse games up a mountain never end well. So long as Lambot is on my tail, I've got him in my pocket.

A left, and a right, and we ride over a wooden bridge, over a stream, and then up – up and further up towards Allos. I memorised the stage map last night before my pre-stage nap, although we've done this before – many years ago – the ride up to Valgelaye is the hardest part of the day, and I've been riding the 44 x 18 which I'll swap out for the 44 x 22 once we peak and hit the descent down to Barcelonette. Lambot will probably do the same, he's just waiting for me to do it first.

What sort of strategy is that? Where's the element of surprise?

All these kilometres, and we barely talk. I ask Lambot what he plans to do after the Tour, to pass the time.

Bike shop, he returns, offering little more.

"What, open one? Or have you already got one?"

He shrugs. "Had one in Antwerp during the war, but… y'know."

Yeah, we all know. The unspoken five-year itch. I have no idea what it was like in Belgium, but some of the other riders said it was a living hell. As we climb, Lambot's opening up.

"Did you ride, y'know, during the war? Did you get out at all?"

He chooses his moments, doesn't he. Just as the gradient hits 20% and we're entering Allos, but why not, let's talk now.

"I didn't, no. Other guys got dispensation – went off to the velodromes. Alavoine, Pélissier, they were competing against Oscar Egg and the others. But I said I didn't want to touch a bike, so they put me in the bicycle unit, mostly carrying out repairs, taking bikes out to the front. They saw I waTs handy. I swore I'd never get on a bike again. Sick of them, sick of the fighting."

"You changed your mind though."

"Yeah. I'd been carrying the folding bikes on my shoulders all winter, and I'd just had enough of carrying it. Once I got on it – that was it. I love the bike."

Lambot's powering on, it's good to actually ride side-by-side for once. "I want to build my own bikes. Lambot bikes. Imagine that!"

I nod. Imagine that, indeed. And a Tour win would double the price.

"Fancy walking for a bit?" I ask.

"Thought you'd never ask."

We push our bikes up the steepest part of the col, careful not to make too much noise for fear of rock slides, just two old men, one in grey and one in an ugly bright yellow jersey, trying to get through the day without too much incident.

Firmin Lambot

I am Death. Warmed. Up.

Christophe has agreed to stop and push the bikes over the top of the Velgelaye. Mercy. The signs say Allos – from here, the descent is going to be life-threatening. Christophe has been banging on about it since we started walking. I almost got on my bike and attacked right there and then.

Do I have a race strategy? Do I have a plan?

Stay on my bike; that will do for today. The day after tomorrow's the Galibier, so let's just get home in one piece.

I follow Eugène down the first drop, and one of Desgrange's men is holding up a sign saying "rapid descent, tight corners. Men have been out all morning sweeping the roads, you can tell – it's slick. We swoop through Martinet and screech to a halt at a hairpin bend, creating that acrid burning smell of brake on rim.

Next thing I know, I'm ahead of him. He took a corner too wide. Now Eugène's screaming at me to go slower, but I don't know how. Gravity is working its spell on me.

There's another man with a sign here, this time "Short descent, careful on the bridge" which obviously means that the bridge is broken. We drop once more, Eugène's still on my tail. This is no place to attaAck so I ease up, brake sharply, and we've got another turn after the bridge. Another man, this time, with a flag – go this way, which means don't go that way, God forbid.

Another wooden bridge. Thud. Thud. Thud. Sounds like a flat, but we've been here before, I remember the sound. Thud. Thud.

And then we drop again. The concentration required, I tell you... brake and find your line for the hairpin, off the brakes for the turn. Eugène is still behind, I can hear him swearing.

Back when Eugène started racing, he was the young gentleman of the Tour. An urbane athlete among yobs. Those men from the first Tours, they'd make a whore blush. Thieving, lying, stealing, cheating, swearing. It was as if Desgrange was giving out points for bad behaviour. Christophe was a breath of fresh air, a role model.

Today, he's the old Gaulois, the crabby veteran who shields the rest of us from the title of old timer, a throwback to the days when riders were emerging from the cheat-fest that was the Tour de France. And he's behind me, swearing his face off like it's 1904. Today, I quite like the guy.

Tomorrow, though...

Stage 10

1	Honoré Barthélémy (FRA)	13h 08' 10"
2	Jean Alavoine (FRA)	+ 12' 19"
3	Firmin Lambot (BEL)	+ 12' 58"
4	Eugène Christophe (FRA)	+ 16' 02"
5	Léon Scieur (BEL)	+ 48' 05"
6	Paul Duboc (FRA)	+ 51' 50"
7	Jacques Coomans (BEL)	+ 1h 16' 57"
8	Jules Nempon (FRA)	s.t.
9	Alfred Steux (BEL)	+ 2h 35' 23"
10	Joseph Van Daele (BEL)	+ 2h 41' 40"

General Classification

1	Eugène Christophe (FRA)	
2	Firmin Lambot (BEL)	+ 23' 19"
3	Jean Alavoine (FRA)	+ 39' 51"

STAGE 11
GRENOBLE TO GENEVA

Honoré Barthélémy

Ah man, me nuggets. Right, I spent last night with me right nugget in a bowl of ice, not nice it was, not nice, and I swore to myself if I make it to the end of this race, I'm seeing a proper doctor, as I've got some money now, quite a lot of it, and this toenail's coming out.

This stage up the Galibier is meant to "sort us out". It's sorting my toenails out, I'll tell you that. First sign of a climb and it's like all the boredom and the pain and the agony of racing on flat roads has gone, and I'm leaving the other riders behind, or rather they're disappearing into the distance.

I didn't even try.

And up the Galibier, man, I thought it would be like in the Pyrenees, where I was the only man for miles, but there were motorbikes and Sunday cyclists and people running alongside me, they're proper crazy, proper mad, it was great. Mr Alavoine would love this, I remember thinking to myself, this is his kind of thing. A proper buzz, a real commotion.

There's some riders who hate the crowds running alongside them, they can't handle the distraction, don't like the fans chatting with them. I love it. There was this one man with a huge moustache who was sweating buckets to keep up with me. Brilliant!

The rest of the Galibier was like that but only more crazy, a manic sweat-lashed, fury-filled rush, and when you reach the top, man, the snow was banked up on both sides and it was blinding with the sunlight and after a while you remembered how cold it was – and how all of a sudden, the crowds have thinned and you're on your own, freezing your fingers off and I'd packed some gloves, Mr Christophe told me I needed them, and I had a newspaper which I put down my jersey.

I try not to read l'Auto, but it comes in handy! Don't tell Mr Desgrange.

And all the sweating you did rushing up the mountain, it starts to freeze and you're pedalling harder and harder to warm your body up, slap your thighs and hope the descent's coming soon, and sure enough it does, and as you fall, the noise from the wind fills your ears with cloud and white noise and you're falling down narrow roads, hairpins and paths, spitting up stones and dancing through the snow. And you could fall off at any moment, go down the mountain head over heels over head over heels over head, and bang - you'd hit the bottom in no time. Better not think like that. And the quicker you go, the colder you get.

I reach Saint-Michel de Maurienne for the checkpoint, and who's there but old Papa Desgrange himself, beaming from ear to ear.

"Honoré, dear boy", he yells above the noise of the crowds, "twenty minutes behind schedule but I'd wager you're twenty minutes ahead of the rest!"

"Is this an interview?" I ask, quite genuinely.

"Haha, dear boy, everything's an interview. It's 8 o'clock, have some breakfast."

There's coffee and croissants, not exactly Machurey's feeding station, but it'll do for now. I nick one for later, stuffing it in my back pocket.

"What's the next one like, Mr Desgrange?" I ask because I forgot to read the preview, and I realise I've still got his newspaper down my front. Slightly awkward. His eyes glance towards it.

"The Aravis? Oh you'll enjoy it, dear boy, you'll enjoy it. Gradients are enough to knock a man backwards off his bike. Just grit your teeth and dream of Paris."

I ride off, and that Mr Desgrange, man, he's a tough nut. Mr Scieur was telling me that he signed up for the war, even though he didn't have to. Wanted to get involved at all costs, even though he was too old. Rolled up his sleeves, so he did, even wrote in the sports paper that everyone should show no mercy to the filthy Prussians, shoot them in the chest if you can, look them in the eye and shoot them in the chest.

And he was a rider and a half. That's why the rest of the field respects him so much, that's why he can tell you a mountain's going to knock you backwards off your bike, or that you need to 'man up' and face a full day in the saddle, because he's done it before, and he fought the Germans at the age of 50.

Mr Desgrange, man. Tough.

Eugène Christophe

Riding with Lambot is like boxing. He's taken my punches, I've taken his, and now I'm waiting for him. He's waiting for me, waiting for my bike to break or my legs to fail. Two old sluggers, that's all we are. On a good year, we'd be on our way home.

Here's a left jab from our Belgian boxer-cyclist, attacking down my left-hand side which I had left open, but the next turn is on the right, he's got to come round which he can't as the gradient suddenly rises. He slumps back down into his saddle and mopes, but it's a warning – and perhaps that's all it was – a warning. Watch yourself Eugène.

The bell goes. A truce, for a short while, as the gradient eases, but soon, around the rocks, and we enter a tunnel. With each metre, the temperature drops another degree, and the cold is taking the edge off Lambot's attacks. But not mine – I land a right hook and Lambot was sleeping. Attack when your opponent is least expecting it. But look at this Belgian – he's out of his saddle, and back onto me before I can catch my breath.

Lucotti is with us, the Italian lad, and he goes off the front himself. I look behind at Firmin and he shakes his head. There's only two boxers in the ring right now, he can fight his own fight, a l'Italienne. We watch him dance off into the distance, half-admiring, half-jealous, two fighters momentarily on the same side, forgetting the combat and lost in the same thoughts.

Another truce, and Lambot points out a spring. I go first. Fresh water, a chance for the old men to fill up the bidons and size each other up. It's icy cold up here, or at least it's icy cold compared to what we've been used to. That makes the water even colder, just what you need after the worst climb of the Tour.

Duboc, the lad from Normandy is with us.

"Hey, apple-boy, those girls are checking you out."

"Wossat? Them three? Hey ladies!" he waves over at them.

They seem to be taking pity on him – he does look a state, to be honest. One of them says "You poor man, you poor poor man," and Lambot's in fits of laughter.

"Me? Poor?" he says, completely missing the point. "I've never been richer – I might look like I'm pissing around on me bike, but I've made 25,000 francs so far. What d'you make of that?!?!"

"Classy," says Lambot, chugging back the spring water.

Ding dong, we're back on. Leave the apple-boy to his ladies. The descent of the Galibier is fierce and fast, Lambot takes the advantage but I've got his wheel. With each hairpin, he's got the acceleration out of the turn, but I'm onto him by the next one, it's a game of cat and mouse, dodging the punches, making your opponent wear himself out. Round 6, the bell goes, more hairpins, more wearing out, but who's wearing who out? You can hardly tell, is it me, making him accelerate, or is it him, making me chase?

All the way down, it's like this, until we hit the start of the Aravis, a climb I've had in mind for days, hoping that the Galibier had sapped Lambot and Alavoine and that I've got reserves in the tank, but something's not right, something's holding me back. It's like a weight has been strapped onto the back of this bike and I'm dragging it along. Lambot's going, he's looking back, wondering why I'm not following, but he's gone and I'm not with him. Punch. Landed.

I'm on the ropes; Lambot's landing jabs and my defences are down. The temperature has risen again since the descent of the Galibier and I'm sweating buckets of cold sweat, my coach is leaning over my shoulder with the towel: "punch the pedals, Eugène, punch the pedals, don't let your cadence drop, think 1, 2, 3, 4, 5, 6, 7, 8…" and Lambot's getting smaller, getting further, going round the corner; he's gone. All I can do is keep my cadence up. Why am I so heavy? Why am I not matching my opponent? This is wrong.

I need a push. Coach, what do I do? Play your own game, keep your head down, dance on your pedals, don't think of your opponent right now, play your own game.

There's a loneliness to a defeated cyclist. You're a dead weight pedalling backwards and all of your energies are focused on shaking off the sluggishness that's overcome you. You're asking yourself questions. Why am I like this? Why have I forgotten how to race? The aches and pains you'd forgotten return and amplify.

Alavoine has gone past me, with a look of concern on his face. Steux is behind him, Scieur not far behind. They're at least riders I can hang on to. All I have to do is play my game, box the way I box, and slowly slowly reel him in.

"What's hit you, Christophe?" shouts Jean-lad.

"Lambot", I groan.

"Took him long enough. Come on, grab my wheel, there's no commissaires for miles."

I do just that. It's at moments like this you're tempted to take the Pélissiers' pharmaceutical fizz-bombs or whatever it is they call them these days. Dynamite. Some of the boys have this ointment for their legs, helps in the mountains so they say but only to keep the cold out. I tried it once, ended up getting some in my eyes and they were stinging for days. Didn't finish the race.

There's a checkpoint, and I'm in a rush, much as Lambot would have been, no doubt. No breaks from here to the finish – if you need the toilet, it's in your pants. This is it, final round – ding dong, the bell's gone, is there life in the Frenchman yet? I sign on with a squiggle, check for Lambot – two minutes advantage he has – two minutes, how did he manage that - and I'm straight back on the bike. The other lads are the same, and we're racing down the Aravis, hairpin upon hairpin. I see him now – he's there, at the bottom, near a bridge. My opponent, in view. It's one versus four – I've got Steux, Alavoine and Scieur. And he's stopped. Here's the impetus – the fightback – the French champion is closing in for the kill. He had two minutes, I can cut it back, most of it if not all of it. He's out of view.

Woosh, this has to be the fastest I've ever come down the Aravis. He's in view. Still farting around with his back wheel. Must be a bad one, and he's looking up. He saw me. Now he's out of view.

The French champion is looking for an angle to land a killer blow, the Belgian is flailing around, another hairpin, another hairpin, and another hairpin – I see him, then I don't see him, I see him, and he's getting back on his bike – I know this part, post-puncture, he'll be easing himself into it, unsure of how it feels, unsure of whether it's the same bike and unsure of whether he can remember how to cycle – it's only fleeting, but that will chop a few seconds off. Another hairpin, come on – here he is, trying to get up to full speed. I see his back. Hunched and grey, every muscle straining at the force of energy going into the pedal strokes. Alavoine is cheering behind me; a few of the other lads join in. This is boxing at its best, the slugger has slugged his way back into the fight – even if his opponent has been caught out on a technicality – the slugger doesn't give up.

I pass Lambot on a right turn, never a wise thing to do but I get away with it, and he settles back into his usual position. Just behind me, to my left, watching me, watching me all the way to the finish line, ready to fight another day, just not today.

The bell goes. The two fighters slump to the canvas and the referee declares it a draw, although morally, we could both claim the win, if we had the heart to argue the point.

I climb off and feel that sqchthch that comes from a long day in the saddle, the sweat and the piss, the mud and the dust, and the pain from the knee injury sustained in Nice, and realise we're in Switzerland, of course we're in Switzerland. I'm struggling to walk, my legs are bowed and my shoes are squirting out blood and mud, was it worth the effort after all? Have I won the Tour at last? With 30 minutes advantage to hold in Geneva, and no more mountain stages, perhaps I actually can win the Tour.

Stage 11

1	Honoré Barthélémy (FRA)	12h 46' 41"
2	Luigi Lucotti (ITA)	+ 10' 08"
3	Jean Alavoine (FRA)	+ 15' 06"
4	Léon Scieur (BEL)	s.t.
5	Eugène Christophe (FRA)	s.t.
6	Firmin Lambot (BEL)	s.t.
7	Jacques Coomans (BEL)	+ 26' 01"
8	Paul Duboc (FRA)	+ 1h 19' 50"
9	Alfred Steux (BEL)	+ 3h 13' 39"
10	Jules Nempon (FRA)	s.t.

General Classification

1	Eugène Christophe (FRA)	
2	Firmin Lambot (BEL)	+ 23' 19"
3	Jean Alavoine (FRA)	+ 39' 51"

STAGE 12
GENEVA TO STRASBOURG

Henri Desgrange

Strasbourg! Alsace! French Alsace!

Ah, now you might be thinking, of course, the Tour must stop in Alsace, especially in 1919, the revival Tour, the year we celebrate the recapture of our own Alsace from the filthy Boche, and yet – and yet – not everyone appears to be 'on side', so to speak.

I am in Belfort, traditionally a stage town, but alas, no more. Their loss, not mine. And I have been accosted by one young man who believes himself to be a fan of the Tour.

"The Tour should stop in Belfort, Monsieur Desgrange, it is vital for the town, for the cycling fans of Belfort, and for our shopkeepers…"

"Shopkeepers? Is that really why you want the Tour to go to Belfort young man? I'll give you shopkeepers – the Tour is not for your shopkeepers and your businesses, it's for France, the nation, the homeland. Not your greengrocers and your boulangers.

"But think, Monsieur, you could create a stage that goes from Belfort to Strasbourg, it would be a spectacle!"

I retort: "A stage of 150km? Have you ever heard the like?"

He has not, but he carries on: "Well, you could zig-zag! And why not miss out the Galibier, the Aravis and the Faucille? That way you could have a stage from Grenoble to Belfort."

All this for Belfort? I pity the boy, weak of mind as he is. 600km of racing, now I would be keen on a stage that long, but only if it had some character, and Grenoble to Belfort, missing out the mountains... well, I see the point of that just as much as I see the point of continuing to argue with this specimen.

"Dear boy, if you'll forgive me, I'm a busy man."

Strasbourg, though! Alsace! French Alsace!

And I am indeed mindful that while for many of us today is indeed a crucial moment in the evolution of our beautiful country, regaining a part of our nation that we thought to have been lost forever, it is not – for everyone – of such importance. To those of us who carry memories of the Prussian invasion of 1871 and the annexation of Alsace and Lorraine, to those of us who lost friends and family, caught on the wrong side of the German lines, this is the stage of triumph, an opportunity for France to show Alsace her best. Yet, to others, born long after the annexation, to those who did not experience the pain first-hand, there is a certain shrug of the shoulders. A certain "on with the show" attitude that, personally, I fail to understand.

And indeed, I do understand – yes, even I understand, that for many in Alsace, being recaptured by France – or should I put it another way – being rightly reallocated to their homeland, is almost a non-event. In many cases, it has happened begrudgingly. I concede, yes, even I concede, that many people in Alsace believe themselves to be German, and admit out loud that they would prefer to carry on speaking German or whatever bastardisation it is that they speak with their forked tongues.

And with the generations, so passes gratitude. Today's Alsatian youth may put on a show of Francophilia tomorrow, but after the Lanterne Rouge has passed, what is to stop them putting back on their lederhosen and dreaming of a return to the heimland? Hm?

This means more to me than perhaps it does to the riders, but in time, this will mean more to the people of Alsace than the liberation itself. For today is the day they become part of the Tour de France, that they are welcomed back into the fold with a spectacle that is quintessentially French.

So on with the show, it is. On with the Tour, and I am more than happy to roll the first dice in the cultural reappropriation of Alsace.

Aha, yes, to the victors the spoils.

On with the show.

Eugène Christophe

Today's preparation has been long in the making. I must attack Lambot at the first available opportunity, and I cannot allow age to stand in the way of an early throwing of the gauntlet. I woke up around midday, and rode around the centre of Geneva for an hour, just to calm the twitching muscles, my soigneur riding closely behind, along with thirty or so curious Swiss fans.

I marvel at this country, in different ways. The respect

for time, so deeply ingrained in their culture, our time keepers for the Tour must choose Geneva specifically for its watchmakers. The cleanliness, too. France is filthy, and not just due to five years' neglect and the bombs of the enemy, it always has been filthy. Here, even the cobblestones appear to have been polished individually.

I returned to the hotel for a small lunch, followed by a stroll, again with around fifty Swiss fans in pursuit, and then back to the hotel for a sizeable dinner – no cheese – my soigneur points out that cheese slows you down, not that it has harmed Lambot, but to each his own. With an hour's digestion carefully planned, around 9pm, it's a short nap of around two hours before supper, and a roundabout bike ride to the Café de la Couronne in the centre of Geneva. Now, I say roundabout – the approach I have taken is to tackle some of the slightly tougher gradients in the town centre, and find some clearer spots for a sprint, back round a couple of times, to really soften up the muscles and get myself in peak condition for the start.

Is it my imagination, or did some Belgian net curtains twitch as I passed the hotel?

At the Café, a band is playing and the Tour officials have held the crowds back from the signing-on table. Desgrange finds these cafés and somehow they always look and feel the same whether you're in the north, the south, or – as it turns out – Switzerland. Gas lights, the smell of stale beer, rubbish band...

Nempon, obviously, has been there since 10 (it is now 1am), and has been nervously sipping at his mineral water, looking at his cheap watch. There's a huge noise erupting from the café as I'm spotted. It takes longer than usual to get through the entrance and reach the desk, but when I do, Desgrange is there with the nervousness of a small dog eagerly awaiting its owner after a day at work.

And then I remember – of course – it's Alsace Day. Desgrange's big day. He doesn't seem to realise it's just another day of brutal hard labour for the rest of us, whether we're arriving in Alsace, Lorraine or Zanzibar. But we all know where we're going. I've got my route map taped to my bar, or at least the key moments and turns, the checkpoints and the feeding points, and I've kept the directions in my back pocket, just in case I get stranded and Desgrange's men forget to hold up the signs. FRENCH ALSACE THIS WAY, they'll say.

We know, we'll say.

54km

The joints are creaking and the knee is flaring up, but the attack has floored Lambot. The Faucille was as predicted - a false contest. Too dark to attack, too cold to think about riding alone. That's a shame because at the right time of day, it would be a beautiful climb; it would be a contest. The checkpoint at Morez was the moment. The sun was coming up over the horizon, Lambot was dawdling towards the back of the pack, no longer hanging off my shoulder, for once miscalculating.

How often does Lambot miscalculate? Probably never.

I lashed the pedals, digging deep into the foot-holders, gritting my teeth. Don't look back, that's the first rule of an attack. Don't turn, you'll lose momentum, and your opponent will know you're on his mind. You need to show him how little he matters to you.

When you're out front, there are no riders to act as targets. That makes it doubly difficult; you're left alone with your imagination and you're wondering – how far behind could he be? What speed would he be going at now? Is he attacking that gradient better than me? How many breaks will he take – or will he take any at all? In the absence of a rider in your line of sight, the mind takes over.

Lambot will have planned meticulously for this stage, but he won't have planned for this attack. Now I've got to plan on the hoof, and imagine the theatre that's unfurling behind me. He'll be pairing up with Léon Scieur, maybe Steux and Coomans if they can keep with the pace. He'll be doing deals – you get this bonus if you ride me up this climb, you get to go through this town first if you protect me from the sidewind. Desgrange hates it, and his commissaires are everywhere, but the art of winning the Tour is partly the art of avoiding the punishment.

Back in 1910, in the Milan-San Remo, I was 90% certain that I was in the lead on the descent into San Remo, but in the weather that day, you couldn't be sure of anything. All the way down I had this nagging doubt that Luigi Ganna had somehow shaken off the icicles and was on my tail. It was like being chased by the invisible ice man. We had walked our bikes over the Turchino Pass in atrocious conditions. Men were collapsing in the blizzard. Van Hauwert, it was who was leading, he had collapsed and was taken into a cottage. They say he refused to come out. I had stomach cramps, so bad that I crumpled into the snow. An innkeeper had dragged me by my shoulders to lie by the fire. It took me at least an hour to recover. He wouldn't let me go – so I lied to him and said I'm abandoning the race.

I was back on the bike, and one of the race commissioners told me that Ganna was about ten minutes behind. So it was with the ghost of Ganna chasing me down the mountain into San Remo that I took off. There was another reason for reaching San Remo, though – not victory, although victory would come sure enough. It was the warmth. Every kilometre further down towards San Remo, the temperature rose by a degree.

And every kilometre that passed, I looked back for Ganna. Still nothing. With Milan San Remo, everything comes down to the last few hundred metres, could he have been stalking me? That descent was fearful for so many reasons.

It was only afterwards I found out that he was being driven down the mountain, and Alphonse, at the time my coach, was trying to block his car down the hairpins, in a valiant attempt to uphold some form of cycling justice. I always liked Alphonse, he stood on the right side of everything. Even tried to have this Tour postponed, for the sake of the riders.

Ganna though… I respected him, but I never liked him. He was your typical 1900s rider – rough, broad-shouldered, worked on building sites, and despite the money and the fame, never stopped reminding you. But for him – and for the Italian riders as a rule – winning was an imperative. It didn't matter how you won, so long as you won. If you had to ride a bike race sitting in the back of your team manager's car, then so be it. Wrapped up in a blanket while the rest of us clanked and shook our bones down dangerous mountain passes, well that would do for Luigi.

Trouble is, with many of these riders, and Luigi is no exception, they never found an honest answer to a difficult question. If the question is – how do you complete the coldest Milan-San Remo ever? The answer is not – jump in a car. That's leaving a job half done. Where's the honour in that? I remembered my cyclocross events, the running with the bike slung over your shoulder, the sudden dips in the ground, the slush and the mud… that's how you win, you learn to ride in every condition and in every situation. Ganna never thought like that. He was a big man, a tough man, but a dishonest man.

And that's what worried me most. A dishonest man, careering down the mountain behind me, perhaps – or perhaps not.

In the end, the not knowing is what gets you as a bike rider.

I don't know where Lambot is, and that's what worries me the most. All these days in the saddle I've looked over my shoulder to find him, in hindsight it was reassuring. Without him, I don't know how to moderate my pace or spare my energy, I've got nothing to react to or provoke, I just have to ride to the maximum of my ability, every pedal stroke.

Léon Scieur

Firmin, you idiot.

Now, go, now! Come on, boy.

If I can't relay with Firmin, I can cajole him. I can coax him out of his stupor, if that's what this is. Eugène has disappeared up the road to La Chapelle des Bois, where this climb ends, and Firmin is hollow-faced, and worst of all, silent.

I've known moments like this with Firmin. Out training around Florennes, we'd ride in silence for hours, the best of friends, enjoying the early spring in Wallonia, the unusual warmth and the crazy quiet. And other days, we'd ride in silence for hours, with Firmin suffering at my side, nothing but the grunt and the wheeze, the occasional 'godverdommer', Firmin's favourite Flemish borrowing, or a sigh.

Today, it's the sound of silence. His mind is elsewhere.

"Stay with me Firmin, stay with me," I shout, giving him a line he can follow. Curves in the road, more bends. It's hard to provide a slipstream for a man who doesn't want one.

He's ambling from one side of the road to the other, a man in search of himself – am I here, am I there, am I anywhere on this road? So I drop back and block the left of the road.

"Anyone there today, Firmin?"

No response. His eyes bore into the road, is he trying to read the road? Is he playing a game we don't know about?

"Dejo, if you've got a strategy, let us in on it."

Still nothing. Could this be a ploy? Come to think of it, we've all done it. Let a rider go off in a breakaway to wear himself out. Save your energies for later in the stage. Or is he hoping that Christophe will be overcome with emotion at arriving in Alsace? So much so that he'll forget to pedal. Far-fetched, perhaps too far for a dreamer like Firmin.

Still nothing. So on we ride, through French border towns that are neither here nor there, neither one thing nor another. I force the pace a little, and Firmin begrudgingly accepts the help he is being given. On days like this, you accept the darker side of Lambot, because he is like these border towns, neither here nor there. Blank, waiting to be drawn on which Firmin will turn up.

There's a checkpoint at Pontarlier. It's a slalom into the town centre, roads full of Tommies and women, young boys in shabby suits. Another of these ambiguous towns – plenty of pretty roads and buildings but what are you? In this time of national certainty, it feels strange to be in borderlands where people have one foot in one country, the other in the next one.

Firmin peels himself off his bike and signs, I can see him checking Christophe's time, muddy sweat dripping onto the table. The commissaire is put out, asks for a rag to clean the timesheets with. My turn; I see that Christophe has three minutes on us.

Eugène Christophe

275km

Alsace. You can imagine Desgrange in his car now, spitting with disappointment at the crowd size.

"Why didn't they come? What a bunch of ungrateful Krauts! Filthy Boche!"

Mulhouse is a ghost town. Barthélémy is behind me, asking which bumhole we're in today, Jean-lad is explaining that it used to be French, then German and now they're trying to be French again. By not turning up.

To be fair, there's a few people in the town centre, probably out shopping for sausages or something and they've stumbled upon a bike race that's going past, so they crane their necks to see these exhausted French cyclists bringing Henri Desgrange's famous circus through town. If they hang around long enough, the Belgians will be along soon.

There's 20 francs on offer if you get past the Mairie first. Jean-lad peels off my wheel and Lucotti races after him. I'm too late to compete, but I'm out of the saddle anyway, perhaps they'll offer something for third place. I've not kept up with who's earned what so far, but in bonuses, Jean's heading for an early retirement.

There's a checkpoint, which is perfunctory – hop-off,

sign, hop-on, no time for niceties or formalities - there's a Belgian train which is on my back. I have no idea where it is, when it's coming, or how big it is, but Lambot's on board, and he's coming for me.

I'm back on, part of the Franco-Italian peloton that has led this stage from early morning. It must be early afternoon now. I missed the timekeeper's watch at the checkpoint in my hurry. Alavoine is leading the charge - I should be wary of Jean-lad, he is within touching distance if I have a mechanical. I don't doubt that he'd be the first to attack if that happens, but for now he's Jean-lad, the dandy, the happy-go-lucky bonhomme du peloton. Funny how a man can wear so many hats on one bike. One snapped chain and the man will become beast.

It's somewhere in the Forest, though. It always is. Two sounds. First, a thud and a chhrrrr, and the ominous sound of wood on road, the feeling that a weight has been applied to the front wheel. One minute you're admiring the smell of pine trees, the next you're burning rubber and scorching your wooden rims as a puncture rings out through the trees.

The second sound? The sound of Walloons in the distance, the unmistakeable sound of Léon Scieur hollering in the background; he's not called the locomotive for no reason. He even comes with an early warning system. And where Scieur goes, Lambot is sure to follow.

I'm off my bike in an instant, the tyre round my shoulders and armpits is called into action, I lift it over my head and throw it to the side of the road. Stand ready, I need you alert, young tyre. A good mechanic needs to change a tyre in less than 4 minutes, and if he can, 3 minutes – that doesn't help me with the Belgian train approaching – but I have no time for self-pity or introspection. I push as much air out of the tyre as I can and it's off the wooden rims in no time. I abandon this one, and the new tyre is on within seconds, but as I reach for the pump, a flash of grey hurtles past, and I know it's the locomotive and his Florennes carriage. There's three of them, so perhaps Steux or Coomans.

Focus.

Why won't the tyre pump quicker? I'm dripping dirty sweat now, Lambot's ahead and I'm flapping.

Air, get in. Push. Push. Push.

It's on. Get the wheel in, Eugène. Tighten it. Test it. Come on, what is it now? 30 seconds? He'll be back in the peloton. A minute? No it can't be that much. Jump on and focus, Eugène, focus.

Alone in the forest, and I have that fleeting thought that I have forgotten how to ride a bike, but yes, yes I can ride a bike, what else have I been doing for the last 300km today? Riders ask themselves the most stupid questions. I wonder if Lambot thinks the same. I wonder if he thought the same coming down the Aravis.

Time to knuckle down. Time to clear the mind.

The hunger comes; I have to fight it. I have some food in the musette, but every movement slows the attack. It's a balancing act, but I reckon I can finish this race without eating.

The only way back to Lambot is consistency. Every movement has to be judged to perfection, like a factory machine. The legs are levers, the lungs are bellows, the pedals the cogs in the machine, Eugène Christophe is on the charge, anger coarsing through my veins the fuel.

I exit the forest, and a long straight road presents me with the sight I need. Lambot and the Belgian train. Out of sight they go again, over a dip. But that's all I need. Give me another sight. A taster.

I'll catch that train.

Henri Desgrange

Strasbourg! Alsace! What a let down.

French Alsace, what you are about to witness, those of you who are present, is nothing less than the manifestation of French athletic prowess. Once my brave, brave riders have entered this town, and have offered up this heroic display of muscle, grit, bravery and determination, you shall have the opportunity to marvel at them – those of you who are present – and you shall remember that not very deep down, you are still French. And we still welcome you back into the fold.

French Alsace.

"Sir, I didn't quite get all of that."

Desmarets. Smart boy, but this requires an expert.

"Bob, dear boy, it's this simple. The Tour has been enthusiastically received by all present here in Alsace. The crowds are enormous, rapturous, even. You do not, by any means, report accurately on crowd size."

"Yes, sir, but won't they read it?"

"Does it matter? It's a matter of perception, Bob, the perception of our readers back in Paris is more important than a few Germans."

"But aren't they French now, sir?"

Yes, Bob. And no. Not yet.

"That's irrelevant. Bob, do your job. Rapturous crowds, happy event, Alsace warmly greets riders, clearly delirious at end of German rule. Etcetera etcetera."

And yet, as we all know, these are not rapturous crowds. Nor are they what you might call 'crowds', they are people, gathered around almost by chance, mystified at this passing show. I have a feeling that we must undertake many more Tour finishes in Alsace to remind these people of their heritage. A mere single Tour, it appears, will not be sufficient. Repetition maketh the Frenchman.

And here come the boys themselves, as I predicted, all together, six or seven of them. Give me a French winner. Give me a story, boys. Give me something.

"Bob, can you get a good view?"

"Absolutely, sir – looks like Jean-lad is at the front with one other."

"One other? Can you be more precise, Bob?"

"I think it's Lucotti, the Italian boy. Yes, it does look like him."

"Who else is with them? Anyone else got a chance?"

"The yellow jersey is there, in third, but I don't think Christophe's going for it. It's just Alavoine and Lucotti. 100 metres to go."

Come on Jean-lad. Come on! Just one more push, Jean-lad. For France, for the homeland. For your country, come on boy! For Alsace! The two are pushing hard, it's a mighty battle as the boulevard widens out.

"Who's got it, Bob?"

"It's close. It's very close, sir. It's Lucotti, sir. Luigi's won it."

Oh bugger.

Stage 12

1	Luigi Lucotti (ITA)	15h 08' 42"
2	Jean Alavoine (FRA)	s.t.
3	Léon Scieur (BEL)	s.t.
4	Firmin Lambot (BEL)	s.t.
5	Honoré Barthélémy (FRA)	s.t.
6	Paul Duboc (FRA)	s.t.
7	Eugène Christophe (FRA)	s.t.
8	Jules Nempon (FRA)	+ 3' 44"
9	Jacques Coomans (BEL)	+ 39' 41"
10	Joseph Van Daele (BEL)	+ 2h 15' 39"

General Classification

1	Eugène Christophe (FRA)	
2	Firmin Lambot (BEL)	+ 23' 19"
3	Jean Alavoine (FRA)	+ 39' 51"

STAGE 13
STRASBOURG TO METZ

Honoré Barthélémy

Watching Mr Lambot today, I now know what I have to do, if I'm to become a top cyclist like him. I have to be cruel. I have to see the other riders not as people, but as machines and I'm a machine just like Mr Lambot.

Mr Christophe had a problem, you see. It was late morning, perhaps 200km gone, and most of us were, tap-tap-tapping out a rhythm on the pedals, lazily coasting along in a happy trance, and Mr Christophe's bike started rattling, and I swear man, I swear blind that Mr Lambot has ears like a bat, finely tuned little ears he's got, and he was bang – off like a shot – and we all went with him, because when one man goes, you go too. Don't you?

And oh, Mr Christophe has a few swear words in him, and they were fading away as we pedalled at a furious pace. Mr Lambot, though, this man is cruel, he's efficient, he's a pure machine. I've been watching him in this race, because in the first stage, he looked like he'd seen a ghost. He was falling off his bike, he was slow, he was pudgy; but then in the second stage, he looked a bit better and in the third, he looked even better. And now he's this colossus of a man, but to attack Mr Christophe on a technicality like that, man, you've got to have a heart of ice.

So here we all are, six of us, led by Mr Lambot and Mr Scieur, cut from the same cloth them two, taking turns at the front as we try to put the knife into nice Mr Christophe, what bad, bad men we are. I feel bad, but I hit the front and take the wind for the guys and think – this is what I have to do. This is who I have to be. A bad man.

Luigi goes next; he's only small so doesn't offer much wind resistance. That's what you need here, a big man, someone like that Belgian Heusghem, who cried off after the first stage, he's about 3 metres tall and 2 metres wide, you could follow him all day and not notice your pedals are turning.

"Mr Lambot," I cry, "can't we let the pace down a little bit? I'm well hurting."

"Nope," he returns, head down into his handlebars.

Mr Scieur's a bit more helpful, "Today, we ride, son. Today, we ride." And he gives me a wink and I can tell this guy's another bad man, because he disguises it with a smile and a wink. Today we ride, man. We rode all day, we rode all night; we rode till Mr Christophe disappeared from sight.

I should be a bad man, too.

And maybe I am. We ride like bad men, and the route is windy and curvy, and the hedgerows are tall, so if the Old Gaul, as they call him, is behind us, he wouldn't know. It's not like other stages where you can see kilometres and kilometres ahead of you; this one is about running on your instincts. He could be minutes behind, he could be seconds, we're just charging forward, relaying and pushing as hard as we can. Bad men.

Finally, a chance to break the rhythm, a checkpoint in a town called Bouley or Boulay, whichever it is, it's a hole, and it was probably a hole before the war, too. Mr Lambot's in no mood to hang around. He leaps off his bike, signs his name in a hurry, and bang, he's back on it. Ah come on, just give us a chance to have some water. Luigi's with me, gives me a nudge, says "Andiamo" which I've learned is Italian for "get a move on, we've got a bike race to ride" so reluctantly I get back on, and we hit the same pace as before.

I'm doing all I can to hang on to the back, these flat stages, man, they're a killer. I know there's a climb coming up soon, not a big one, but I'm going to do the switch on the back wheel just before it, I've got it all planned – trouble is so have all the others – so it's going to be a case of who switches first.

"Thought you could get away, did you?" comes a shout from behind.

It's Mr Christophe! Uh-oh. Teacher's back.

The pace starts to slacken. Mr Lambot sighs, and relaxes back into his usual posture, and the other guys seem to breathe a sigh of relief.

"Fuckers," he mutters, as he accelerates to the front of the peloton.

We ride along like naughty schoolboys who have been playing truant all day. I feel bad, man, really bad. Is it bad that I feel bad? Mr Lambot just looks resigned, like there's no way he's going to win this Tour, because Mr Christophe he just keeps pinging back at him, every time he thinks he's got away, there's the Old Gaul, muttering obscenities and complaining about his dodgy knee, but still there, always there.

And then, what does the Italian do? Luigi, why are you dropping off the back?

Ah, he's changing his back wheel. Switching it round for the climb ahead. Do I do it now? Do I not? What do I do?

None of the others are changing – is that because it's not the right time? Maybe Luigi's got it wrong. I ask Mr Christophe.

"Shouldn't we be flipping our wheels? What do you think?"

"Mebbe," he mutters, still in a mood with all and sundry.

So he pulls up to the side of the road, and rather than attack, so does Mr Lambot. So I do the same, and nobody seems to be in much of a hurry to change. I'm yanking at the chain, filthy hands, that's going to get all over my handlebars, nice.

And who goes past but Luigi? That cheeky Italian. You go, boy, you go!

I'm back on, and I'm the first after him. Haha! Race on!

Mr Christophe is charging up the road behind me, but Luigi was right, he tricked us all. Nobody thought Luigi would have a plan, but he did, the clever little Italian, he knew all along. And here's that climb – up, up, up we go. Wahey!

"Eh, Luigi, you planned that didn't you?"

He looks at me as if to say "I don't understand your words, but I understand your premise, young Honoré Barthélémy, and you are absolutely right."

And I nod and say "well played."

Let's go, then.

But Mr Christophe is back on us again. And now it's the three of us.

"That's some game you've got going there, Luigi," he shouts. "Don't do it again, huh?"

And Luigi smiles again, like he understands but he doesn't. And then he attacks, taking us both by surprise. I look at Mr Christophe. He looks at me. We both go,

France 2, Italy 1, and we catch him and I look back and there's no one in the distance.

"You're going to win this Tour, Mr Christophe. I think Mr Lambot's blown a gasket."

"Serves him right after today," he says, all surly and grouchy, some days he's like that, and I look down and there's blood congealed down his legs and there's bruises and he's sweatier than usual. It's funny because sometimes you don't stop to look at the other riders, you just think they're experiencing the pain the same as you, but Mr Christophe, he's wearing it for the rest of us. He pulls his cap down further over his eyes, fixes his goggles, and ploughs into the oncoming dust.

We're not bad men, we're not good men, I'm not sure what we are, but we're not like other men.

Firmin Lambot

He's gone. Christophe has gone.

Fucking hell. He's getting away. Dejo, Dejo, you fool. Act now. Legs, act.

They won't. They won't react. Fuck, fuck, fuck.

He disappears around a corner, hedgerows blocking my view of him. I've lost sight. Shit. Where's the yellow? Where did he go?

I'm sweating buckets, forcing the pedals down as hard as they'll go, and still I'm getting nowhere. Two stages back I only had to touch the pedals and the bike would fly.

"Firmin, head down."

It's Van Daele.

"What do you mean 'head down', I have to catch him."

He shakes his head. "No, you can't catch him. Put your

head down and ride."

"Is that your race strategy?" I spit, having hardly seen him for the last three weeks.

"Yes. Since you asked," and he looks offended. "Do you actually want to win this race?"

Do I have to answer that? He glares at me, so it looks like I do.

"Yes, OK. Yes, I do want to win it."

"So accept the loss, just minimise it."

Accept the loss and minimise it. Race, but don't race. He's right, and I know he's right. If you can't respond to an attack, you have to round off the edges of your defeat and save something for the next day. We all know what's coming in two days' time, nobody wants to bust a gut when Metz-Dunkirk is looming.

So I wince, and I bite my lip, and put my head down.

"See?" he says. "Stay in it."

I nod. "Sorry."

"It's OK, Firmin," he smiles. "Could be worse."

It could, I agree. It could be stage 14. You look ahead, at Metz in the distance, at the sinewy roads leading down the valleys and up the hills, and beyond only Metz, only grey skies. Somewhere in between, a yellow jersey is pounding his way through villages and town squares, and somewhere behind, two Belgians in grey are hanging on by a thread.

It's only when hope is diminishing that pain increases. Hope is the cyclist's drug, it gets you over mountains, it gets you through cuts, gashes and bruises; it pushes you through sidewinds. But when you start to lose hope, your body lapses. A pulled muscle here, a seeping wound there. A headache here and a backache there. Damage limitation is a painful game.

"10km to go, Dejo," barks Van Daele.

The modern cyclist is also a mathematician. You won't have found Aucouturier calculating km/h differences in his head, he'd have been punching into the wind like the barrel-chested numbskull that he was, win or bust. So if Christophe is halfway between here and Metz, that's 5km, and he'll be riding at 25km/h, while I won't be pushing much more than 22km/h.

Work that one out, Hippolyte.

Trouble is, I know Christophe better than any other rider. I've watched his every pedal stroke for days on end. I've eaten with him; I know his every injury. I should know how to beat him by now, and it kills me that I haven't found his weakness yet. I should know his weakness, because he's more like me than I ever cared to admit.

Stage 13

1	Luigi Lucotti (ITA)	11h 55' 13"
2	Honoré Barthélémy (FRA)	s.t.
3	Léon Scieur (BEL)	+ 2' 04"
4	Eugène Christophe (FRA)	+ 2' 49"
5	Jacques Coomans (BEL)	s.t.
6	Firmin Lambot (BEL)	+ 7' 35"
7	Joseph Van Daele (BEL)	s.t.
8	Jean Alavoine (FRA)	+ 12' 27"
9	Paul Duboc (FRA)	s.t.
10	Alfred Steux (BEL)	+ 2h 17' 42"

General Classification

1	Eugène Christophe (FRA)	
2	Firmin Lambot (BEL)	+ 28' 05"
3	Jean Alavoine (FRA)	+ 49' 29"

STAGE 14
METZ TO DUNKIRK

Eugène Christophe

Today was the day I lost the yellow jersey. And with it, the Tour.

What started out as a 30-minute lead ended up as a 2-hour deficit. Lambot's Tour, and he never even knew it.

We had spent the day hunkered down in the hotel. The soigneurs moved quietly from room to room. The rain battered against the windows as riders made silent prayers, make it stop, make it stop. We lunched in silence, only Nempon failing to break the omerta, the secret vow that all riders ahead of a monster stage like this adhere to. But what would Nempon know? He's an amateur on an ill-fitting bike.

For the rest of us, our hardest day's work was to come, and no matter how much food you filled your stomach with, it couldn't replace the fear and the dread of what was to come.

I went around the back of the hotel to tinker with my bike, for lack of anything else to do. Lambot and Scieur were there, saying nothing, just adjusting their gears, checking their headsets.

I held the route map against the wind. Not only was this stage to be the hunger stage, it was to be multiple stages rolled into one. A Desgrange special, twisted and cruel. Lorraine up first, with its hills was bound to be technical and would require a smaller gear, but once we hit the cobbles, you need to use your power. A 44 x 18 to start the stage, a 44 x 20 to end with, then.

I took to my bed after that and dozed off in fitful bursts.

One by one, riders started filtering out of the hotel, collecting bikes from Alphonse, collecting musettes and supplies. Tyres, baguettes, spanners, rain jackets.

"Not long left, Cri-Cri," he offered. Yes, Alphonse. Not long.

To the café, then. A run-down brasserie once more, the Café Francais et des Halles. The band was playing, pints were swaying, riders were praying. You sign on, you take your obligatory encouragement from Papa Desgrange, you leave, you find your bike, you wait. And you wait. And the rain lashes you harder, as inside, the band plays on, the beer flows, the people cheer and you hate them. You hate them for not caring, for not even knowing, and how would they ever know? You hate them for smiling, for daring to be happy. Wretched souls.

We stood at the start line, our jerseys soaked through before we'd even started, watching the revelry in gaslight. I hate cycling fans. If they were cyclists, they'd have been out there with us at that moment, glumly anticipating their fate like men about to be sent over the trenches. How can you escape the war when everything around you reminds you of the war? It didn't rain every day during the war, but now the only memory you have of those four years of hell is rain, mud and disease, and it comes pouring back as you return to the scene of the fighting. Desgrange sure has a funny way of helping the nation get back on its feet.

And you ride in the dark, keeping an eye on both sides because even Alavoine harboured hopes of finding the extra time on me today, but Lambot... it was his last chance.

I'd ridden side by side with this man for over a week. I'd heard his munching, his moans, his groans. I'd attacked on his punctures, and he'd attacked on mine. I'd heard him complaining, I'd even heard him not complaining. We were like a married couple, inseparably bickering until one gets the upper hand and the other skulks off waiting for the next opportunity to fight.

I was right about Lorraine. Technical, with some sharp ascents, dangerous descents, but it was also too early for it to have any impact. That's the problem with many stages in one, we're all waiting for the same stage. So we stuck together, shaved a couple of kilometres per hour off the speed and we bided our time.

By late morning, we were still all together. Sick of each other, but rotating the order so that at least some of us could stay dry. Maubeuge was, as it always is, grey and wet, bombed-out and derelict. The mist and the drizzle formed a barrier that we as a peloton took on together, arching ourselves into the thin wall of rain. Lambot, Scieur, Steux, Lucotti, Vandaele, Alavoine, Duboc, Coomans, Barthélémy, myself, into the grey we went.

If you listen, the north has a particular noise. A constant shhhh of rain hitting stone. I swear the rain would still have a noise all of its own even if it didn't hit the ground. The sound of raindrop clashing against raindrop must be infinitesimal, but I'm convinced it makes some kind of sound.

And then I made my first mistake. I could have peed in my trousers, I should have peed in my trousers, but I stopped to answer the call of nature. In hindsight, I still wonder about this moment. The smell of wee is a sign to the peloton that you're a desperate rider. Some men believe a urine-soaked rider to be a threat. After all, if he's ready to wet himself, what more might he try?

As I let my guard down, Lambot went on the attack. "The old man's cracked," he hollered, and he went off the front of the peloton. One by one, men reacted, pulled out of their stupor. Shit – we have to race – and I was just settling in.

I could have got back on, but I needed to pee, and I figured every man has a wee break.

And it was one of those wees that never seems to end. The more you need to get back on your bike, the more you wee. A never-ending stream of piss, steam dissipating in the mizzle, and you imagine you're filling pots, and each pot is 10 seconds. In hindsight, it may have been a quick one, but at the time it wouldn't end.

Did I know then that I was in trouble? No, I'd been attacked before. I'd chased and hunted them down before. I could do it again.

Did I know then that the witch was on my tail? I feared it.

I got back on, alone, and raced hard. Alone, again, alone with my thoughts. Lambot must have what – two minutes? Three at most. That's manageable, and I can make up the three if I find a groove on the cobbles. Alone it will be easier, as I won't have to negotiate my way through with other riders. It's still my Tour, I thought, at the time. It's still my race. The cobbles will be kind.

And when they came, they came hard. The first sector came and I was instantly thrown to the left. You seek any kind of solace, a gutter at the edge or the crown of the cobbles which is slightly more forgiving, untouched by cart wheels, the only traffic seen on these tracks outside of idiots like us racing for glory or money. You watch your front wheel and you look four, maybe five cobbles ahead, judging whether to flex your wrist or not, soften your grip or not, tighten your grip or not, swerve a gap or not, close your eyes or not, hope or not.

This is how they race in the north. Every second is a minute. Every minute is an hour. Your arms are beaten up, vibrations dull your other senses, and you lose momentum with every pedal stroke, only to find it again through sheer willpower and the desire to stay upright. Only speed and brute strength can get you through each sector of cobbles. You swallow mud and you wipe grit and slime from your goggles, if the rain doesn't wipe it off for you.

Oh for some Belgian blood right now.

My wheels were skidding and sliding over the mud. Each patch of cobbles like an ice rink, brown with puddles filling the gaps where cobbles have been taken out. Hit one, you're gone. This is a stage for those who can handle a bike. My cyclocross days come in handy up here.

Sector after sector of cobbles came and went. This is easy, I thought to myself stupidly. This is bone-shakingly easy.

I entered Raismes. The town seemed so innocent at the time. A suburb of Valenciennes, which was a suburb of Lille, it was barely aware of the Tour. Red-brick, grey-sky, sad-eyed Raismes was a nothing sort of a town that most riders wouldn't have noticed. Lambot probably didn't notice Raismes. I can tell you now, there were miners drinking at the bar. Their wives were peeking out of the windows, twitching the net curtains. Kids were playing football.

I noticed Raismes.

There was a level crossing and a town square, a few

piles of rubble and smashed windows. So many aching memories live here. Soon Raismes would be a distant memory.

Then the handlebars dipped from under my hands. A centimetre or two, no more, but enough to alarm me. I started to lose control, jerking to the right, to the left. No no no no no no no no, this can't be happening, not now, this can't happen now.

In the distance, I swear, the laughter of a witch. The Chorchelle d'Arenberg, risen from her pit.

It wasn't just a fork. It was both forks, the wheel hanging stupidly from what remained of the cracked forks. No simple repair, this was the end.

Desgrange had been following. I never knew. The first I realised was his scream from the passenger seat of the Brasier. The punching of the dashboard. The cursing, so unlike Desgrange; maybe he wanted me to win after all.

Quick, I thought. Quick, cycle through the scenarios. A blacksmith. A forge. Heat. How am I going to repair this bike and get back to Lambot? Surely Jean-lad would hang back and wait for me. We'd relay, cut the gap down to something respectable like 30 minutes and then hope for the best on the run-in to Paris. Or that's it – the bike's finished, there is no forge, there's no way of finding a fire with the heat to repair both forks. It can't be done. I'd have to quit.

The mind accelerates the moment the body slows. Find help. Find someone.

A boy, no more than 12 years old:

"Eh mishter, you'll no ge' far on tha'".

Come to, Christophe. The land of the Ch'ti. Work it out.

"You're going to have to repeat that in French, lad."

"Thi'ch way", he jerked at my mud-soaked jersey. I

followed, of course. What else was there to do.

I was back in 1913. The Tourmalet, the minute I realised I wasn't a machine, I was a man with a machine. A civilian. A curiosity. A man carrying a broken bike, following a 12-year-old boy in a nowhere suburb of Valenciennes. That's all I was, at that moment. The same man who followed the road down the Tourmalet to Sainte-Marie de Campan.

There's a train station in Raismes. Who'd have thought it.

You notice everything. Opposite the station, the rue du Marais, number 4, a large red-brick building, riddled with lace curtains. On the left-hand side, a bar. To the right, Persiaux-Chardon: Mechanics. To the right of that, a door with no sign. The boy was leading me to Persiaux-Chardon, passing by the bar with its thirsty miners holding up the zinc, ogling the mudman with a broken bike.

There is a choice here, I thought to myself as the owner of the premises approached. I give up. I give him my number 46, I go to the bar, and I join the miners for a drink. Or I carry on. But of course, I carried on, I always do; that mentality drummed into me from such an early age: you never leave a job half done. The first yellow jersey ever in the Tour de France, leaving a job half done. I shouldn't have thought so. You didn't give up in 1913, you're not going to give up here.

Léonard Persiaux it was who took me into the workshop. A well-built man, square shoulders, fine moustache, I'd have worn one not dissimilar a few years ago. My Joseph Bayle, six years on. There were similarities, sure – the look of amused bemusement in the eyes, the wonder at the very idea a man would cycle this far.

Four or five men, hunched over their worktops, acknowledge me with their eyes. They're working for the railway here; they'll never be out of work. Through the workshop we went, to the back where Léonard Persiaux pushed an iron door into the courtyard. In the corner, a forge, of all things, right here in Raismes, a forge. No Elie Bede here, no following a girl to the edge of town to find a smithy. It's right here.

"Give me your bichycle, I'll sort that out for you," he offers, holding out his hands.

"It's against the rules, you can't."

"What rules?"

"Go ask those three over there," I pointed towards Michel, Desgranges and Baugé, the three musketeers who have solemnly been traipsing in my wake.

"Ahh. Ch'o tell me, in what way can I ach'ich't you?"

"If you can lend me your equipment, I should be able to take it from here."

"Very well," he said, gesturing for one of his helping hands to approach.

I stoked the fire, and took one of the rods on hand, leaving it to one side. That will come in handy. I snapped off the broken forks, cast them to the side, and started to work, filing down the spare rods, filing until they seemed like they'd fit but they wouldn't, they were the wrong size, so I started again, and I filed again.

Desgrange had gone, abandoned me. That says a lot. I glanced up at the clock, ten past one. Léonard Persiaux brought coffee, via his daughter Julia, with a waffle which was meant to be for his daughter Suzanne. I remember thinking – this is a good man – I would do well to impress him today, if this cycling career were to end, as it may. Today.

I overheard Baugé explaining that I was a locksmith by trade, Persiaux making approving noises in the background. I remember Baugé in 1913, the man who tried to convince the commissaires that they should turn a blind eye to the boy with the bellows. And I remember the hell of 1913, the hammering and the filing, the intensity of the heat. This seemed easier.

I entered my world again. I forgot Lambot, for a while. I forgot Jean-boy and Desgrange, I even forgot about cycling. There's a pleasure to be found in monotony, the repetitiveness of a task that must result in perfection and nothing else. I suppose that's why we ride a bike. To emulate the workshop.

The repair, done in under an hour, was impeccable. A work of art. To have carried out the repair at such speed, under such pressure, is something I will be proud of to my dying day. I was not, it seems, alone in marvelling at the job.

"Tha'ch a ch'uper job you'ch done, if you'z want, I'z take you on a'ch a foreman."

I had no idea what he was saying.

Alphonse translated: "He said when the race is over, he'd like to offer you a job as foreman in his workshop. He doesn't believe cycling is a proper career."

"Goodbye, Monsieur Persiaux. And merci."

"A l'arvoyure!"

The Persiaux family waved me goodbye as I got back on my bike, Suzanne whose waffle I had devoured, waving her white handkerchief. I swore I'd return with pudding one day.

And that sureness, that feeling of knowing your bike, had gone. It may only have been a millimetre out from where it was, or it may have been exactly the same, but it didn't feel like my bike any more. It held, sure enough it held, but my feet were no longer turning, not like they were turning this morning. My legs felt like they had never raced before, my calves as if they had never learned how to pedal.

"Have you seen Alavoine?" I screamed at the crowds along the road. "Alavoine?"

Nothing.

Jean-lad, where are you now?

The cobbles in a town are always easier than the farm tracks outside of town, but they still hurt. Another level crossing, and the wheel went from underneath me. Fall left, not right, fall left, don't fall right.

I fell right, of course, right on my smashed-up knee. Another victory for the Chorchelle d'Arenberg, the local witch, the same witch, I don't know which witch, but she's had her fill today. Still another 120km to go, as I heaved myself back into the saddle, and headed for Lille, slowly. All around me, the remnants of a race long since passed. Crowds had dissipated, if they had ever been there.

It was in Lille that I discovered the true extent of the damage. A checkpoint, respectfully silent, silent because nobody knew what to say to me, nobody knew how to articulate any sentence that could possibly have alleviated my suffering and my hurt on learning that it was 5:19 in the afternoon, and Firmin Lambot had passed through here two hours, 25 minutes earlier. On his way to victory.

Jacques Coomans was hanging around. A quiet, pipe-smoking, bulldog of a man, just the type of man you need when there's nothing to say, nothing to be said, but if you're going to be lonely, be lonely together. We nodded to each other, and set off for Dunkirk, knowing that we still had to negotiate over 100km of blinding pain, hitting the cobbled sectors of Bourghelles, Cysoing, Bouvines, the worst of the worst, the most painful of the most painful. And to rub it in, back into the war zone, the ravaged towns, the burned-out farms, tree trunks blackened and split in two, towns and villages that are no more, desolation everywhere you looked, a view to match my mood.

Coomans, my Saint Bernard, led me on. In this hour, a friendship was born, a friendship born in silence, an act of brotherhood; two men battered by the hunger stage, ill fortune, injury, and despair. The rain, incessant, but only there when you thought about it.

As I slowed, so did Coomans, instinctively. As I struggled, so did Coomans. We weed together behind a barn without exchanging a word. We ate by the roadside. We nodded, we got back on our bikes, slowly. There's no rush any more. Coomans' Tour was all about getting to Paris in one piece. Mine, I was slowly accepting, had fallen apart beyond all hope of rescue.

On we rode into the evening, watching grey skies darken, the lights – where there were lights – flickering into life. Gas lamps lit in dark, dank houses, filled with families whose suffering I cannot match, yet this personal calvary went on. No more cobbled sectors left, but roads that led you into traps, potholes that led you into further potholes, Jacques leading me on. Did he wait for me at that checkpoint? Did he know what was happening? He never did say.

And then, after hours of hard labour, pedalling into brick wall after brick wall, Jacques and I encountered the first signs for Dunkirk. The thought that this day might soon be over only made the pedalling worse. It seemed to slow time down. Now it was Jacques who was struggling, his hunched frame slumping deeper into his handlebars. For hours now, Jacques had been leading me home, now I returned the favour, wincing and gritting my teeth. We must have been doing no more than 15km per hour, if that, and word must have got around Dunkirk that I had broken my forks, and had lost the Tour. Men and boys ran alongside us, shouting their encouragement. For every ten metres we cycled, another group of men and boys joined until we were a peloton, in the dark, Jacques and I and hundreds of boys, men and even women, running alongside us, running with us, encouraging, and I felt a welling up in my heart and my eyes. These people, they came to see me, they came to see the Tour. I've lost everything today, I'll never win the Tour, and yet they came to see me home. Along the sea front, they ran, we cycled, we cycled to keep up with them, they ran to keep up with us. Allez, Cri-Cri, we love you, we need you, Allez Cri-Cri.

The end in sight, but nobody was there. Just a mass of raucous cycling fans and two over-tired cyclists slowly approaching the stage finish and as far as I could see, it was unmanned. But the noise had brought people out of restaurants, had brought them out of houses. Word really had got round. Everyone already knew.

Bazin, the Tour's timekeeper, was running from another direction. It's so late, he had given up and gone back to the hotel. Papers in hand, rattling in the rain. The last ten metres were the hardest of all.

It was 9:40 when we reached the line. Bazin, true to his role as always, read out place and time. "Tenth. Eugène Christophe, La Sportive, in 23 hours, 33 minutes and 25 seconds. Eleventh. Jacques Coomans, La Sportive, same time. It's over."

And it was over. But for one last ceremony. A final ritual.

I wrenched myself free of the bike, wheeling it to the Hotel des Arcades, propping it up against a railing. Poor thing. I focus so much on my suffering, I never stop to think about the bike until it's over. What suffering she has been through today. New forks, though. They'll hold.

I squelched up the steps, casting a glance at the menu,

and through the window, I saw Desgrange, Baugé, Cazalis, Michel, and an empty seat, perhaps for Bazin. Turbot with Hollandaise sauce, boiled potatoes. I didn't catch dessert.

I dragged myself through the lobby, stopping to ask for Lambot's room. 152, first floor; turn left, then right. I looked at the stairs. Why stairs? Can't we all just sleep on the ground floor? The carpet felt odd, too. After what seemed an age, I found room 152 and knocked on the door. A grumbled Flemish expletive; the door was already open anyway.

"What happened to you?" Lambot was half-asleep. Bathed. In bed. And I remembered, he speaks in French, he swears in Flemish. Belgians. I'll never make sense of them.

Me, I had no words. They would come out broken anyway. I lifted off my jersey, my yellow jersey I'd held since Sables d'Olonnes.

It was no longer a yellow jersey. It was red, with blood. Brown with mud. Black with coal. But it was a yellow jersey, somewhere underneath. And now it's Lambot's.

I couldn't look at his face. I couldn't look for a reaction, I didn't want to hang around any longer. Just find me my room, find me my bed, find me a way out of here. I turned and left, and the world opened up and swallowed me whole.

26th July 1919

I woke up around 9. Or 10. I don't know. I was still in my cycling gear.

Or did I even sleep at all? I was lying on top of the sheets, still in my shoes, ruminating, replaying the incident in Raismes as if thought alone could alter the past. Shards of light ripped through the curtains and outside, of course, it was raining again. I gave the porter 5f for the newspaper. Until the paper arrived, I couldn't be sure it wasn't all a bad dream. I needed the confirmation.

And confirmation it was, I had started the day 30 minutes ahead of Lambot, I ended it in third place, over three hours behind him. Three hours. I'd lost 70 minutes at Persiaux-Chardon. That's another two hours that Lambot had stolen on me along the way.

A bad day, then.

Alphonse is sitting opposite me at the little table against the hotel bedroom wall. There's no room for two sets of hands, so we fumble uncomfortably and he concedes, retracting his bony fingers back below. He's finding the words hard to find. I break the silence.

"I'll never win the Tour, Alphonse. Never. I think that's pretty obvious now."

"Come, Cri-Cri, you're the best bike rider out there, give it some time, enjoy the cyclocross season, you'll be back next spring with every chance."

"Pfft" is all I can offer. I have no desire to get back on my bike. Even to ride to Paris for the final stage.

"And you're a rich man, now, Eugène."

"How am I a rich man? I lost the Tour, I might not even hold on to third place at this rate."

"The local newspaper has organised a fund in your name. Henri's fuming he didn't think of it first, but he's going to do the same and claim it was his idea. You want to know who's just donated?"

I'm taken aback, speechless. Why would anyone give up what little money they have for me? The country's broke.

"Go on," I say because I think Alphonse wants me to say it.

"Baron Rothschild himself."

"Fuck. Off."

"The very same, and we've had money pouring in to our offices. You are going to be a very rich man indeed, Cri-Cri."

I am stunned. "Where is Desgrange? Why hasn't he stopped by?"

"Devastated, he didn't even turn up to the ball held by the Mayor last night. Couldn't face it."

"Are you serious?"

"You were his favourite. Seems you're everyone's favourite now."

With that, he's off, bids me farewell, relaxing day and all that. I return to l'Auto, and Henri's depiction of the damned man, the unluckiest man in cycling, a man vanquished by the elements and ill fortune. Desmarets, it seems, has contributed, offering 'glory in defeat' which is preposterous. There is no glory in defeat, surely? What's glorious about taking 23 hours to complete a stage?

And yet as the day moves on, the money rolls in. Desgrange, who appears to be affected by the turn of events as much as me, appears mid-afternoon, announcing a flood of donations in my name, from young boys who had run alongside Jacques and me into Dunkirk, to old ladies in the Midi, soldiers in the North, and even a homeless man who offered 2 francs.

As the story develops, so does his mood. I've known Henri since my first tour in 1904. Riders were different back then, rougher round the edges. We needed corralling, nurturing, we needed discipline. But as our sport has evolved, so has Henri. There's nuance where once there was absolute. There's flesh where once there was bone. This Henri, the Henri we know now, is more of a front than many of the younger riders might imagine. The Henri of yesterday would never have let Jean-lad hang onto the car on climbs. He'd have chucked us all out of the race on whatever pretext, even if it meant no rider made it to Paris.

"Eugène, my Eugène, you are rich, my boy, rich!"

"It's just money, Henri, get over it."

"Cri-Cri, tomorrow evening, you will ride into Paris a hero – I dare say that you have a long career ahead of you still. Velodrome contracts will be pouring in after this."

"I don't do velodromes, Desgrange. Quit fucking around with me and admit you're enjoying this. Profiting from it too, I'd guess."

He does that disapproving look he reserves for downbeat cyclists. "Now, don't be like that Eugène."

I'll be however I want to be. I'll ride into Paris for one final humiliation and then I'm done with cycling. I'll hand down my bike, I'll return all the money, and I'll work for Persiaux-Chardon as a foreman, just as Monsieur Persiaux had offered. A job, a real job, not like this stupid fucking cycling career.

Stage 14

1	Firmin Lambot (BEL)	21h 04' 27"
2	Léon Scieur (BEL)	+ 6' 43"
3	Joseph Van Daele (BEL)	+ 17' 08"
4	Luigi Lucotti (ITA)	+ 57' 46"
5	Jean Alavoine (FRA)	+ 1h 31' 39"
6	Paul Duboc (FRA)	s.t.
7	Honoré Barthélémy (FRA)	+ 2h 45' 46"
8	Jules Nempon (FRA)	s.t.
9	Alfred Steux (BEL)	s.t.
10	Eugène Christophe (FRA)	+ 2h 28' 58"

General Classification

1	Firmin Lambot (BEL)	
2	Jean Alavoine (FRA)	+ 1h 53' 03"
3	Eugène Christophe (FRA)	+ 2h 00' 53"

STAGE 15
DUNKIRK TO PARIS

Firmin Lambot

It's like someone has died.

When Christophe turned up at the start line, all conversations stopped dead in their tracks. A couple of lads looked away. Jules Nempon nearly broke out in tears.

After a couple of minutes fiddling with his back wheel, Christophe struggled back up to his feet, and berated us.

"Fucking cyclists," he fumed. "You never know what to say. It's just a fucking bike race."

So that's how we knew he wasn't over it yet. He went back to his bike.

The first ten kilometres or so, if Christophe rode to the left of the road, we kept to the right. And vice versa. I felt like shit for wearing the yellow jersey. I felt like shit for Christophe.

We're just outside Calais, and Christophe has already dropped off the back with a puncture. None of us attacked it hard, we just pedalled on at the same pace; he's not a threat any more.

"Feeling bad about it?" muses Coomans.

No I am not. I shake my head.

"I wouldn't either," he continues.

"Why should I? What's wrong with winning?"

He looks like he's considering this, and then he drops back and smokes his pipe.

I won't show it to the other riders, but I do feel bad about winning. I wanted to win, but I wanted to win by being the better cyclist. Don't we all?

I do believe I have been the better cyclist. I read the papers, I heard Desgrange this morning; Christophe spent 1 hour 10 minutes in the forge, and he still finished three hours behind me. So that's 1 hour 50 minutes between us regardless. I rode like a dog, pissing in my pants so I didn't have to take breaks, alone into headwinds with no protection. I rode faster than I've ever ridden. My perineum hurt so much yesterday I had to keep a pillow between my legs the whole day. My muscles are ripped to shreds, my eyes are stabbing with pain from lack of sleep, and I'm hungry, again.

I started this Tour having barely even touched my bike, let alone sat on the saddle, and I've ended it in the best physical condition of my life. I was a prisoner of the Germans for four years, and I've just won the Tour de France spending nearly ten full days pedalling. Pedalling sometimes like I was riding through treacle, sometimes like I was hitting a wall repeatedly. But I still won it. Not just won it, but I've won it by a mile. But do I feel like I've won it?

By default. So yes, perhaps I do feel bad. I don't feel bad for Christophe, I feel bad for me. Christophe must have known that his bike was likely to break at some point. Old Peugeots are known for their flaky forks, but riders kept riding them because Peugeot paid them so well, back in the day. Whoever wins the Tour is the one who stays upright the longest.

And now Christophe is the hero, and I feel like the villain. Perhaps it would have been better to be the valiant loser.

Talking of valiant losers, here goes Nempon, the home town boy, taking in the adulation of the Calaisiens. Arms aloft, he's pulled into the crowd by some family members, so we all stop.

"Some amateur, that lad," says Alavoine. "Still riding a J-B Louvet bike and eating from Papa Desgrange's top table, though."

"It's a good bike, that," I nod.

He nods back. "Have you noticed it's the wrong size for him?"

I hadn't noticed so I squint to have a closer look. "You're not wrong… how long has he been riding like that?"

"The whole month. We didn't have the heart to tell him."

Jean-boy. I'll miss this lad when we've all gone our separate ways.

Nempon is done and we roll casually out of Calais, sucking Nempon back up into our mini Peloton and spitting him out the back with the disdain he deserves.

It's wild around here. Frontier country. A good place to end a Tour. Sangatte, Wissant… it's like Belgium, but a Belgium that people don't care about. Scorched grass everywhere you look, and the wind carries the waft of dead bodies and burnt tar. There's an unspoken rule in this race when this happens: you don't speak, you don't attack. It's not so much a respect for the dead as respect for the other riders, carrying the weight of the memories they can't shake off.

We're back on the coast, but the rain and the storms from the first few stages have finished and we're left with clear blue skies, a cooling wind, and a view of the

Channel as we crest each hill. The 8 of us go up, the 8 of us go down, the 8 of us ache and the 8 of us count down the minutes to Paris and the end of this Tour.

As we approach Boulogne, there's a drunken mob baying up ahead. It's not even breakfast time, and they're breaching the peace. It's only when we get closer, I realise they're Belgians. And they're chanting my name. Lambot, Lambot, Watch Him Go, Lambot!

I'm showered with Lambic as I pass. It's better than some of the other substances we've been showered with.

"NOW do you feel like you've won?" shouts Alavoine, stopping to ask for a bottle of his own.

Eugène Christophe

Duboc: "You ready?"

"Not really."

"The noise is for you, Cri-Cri. Not me."

I shrug. I'm not ready for this. I should or could have been here thirty minutes ago. I should or could have been wearing Desgrange's awful yellow jersey.

Should haves and could haves are all I have. And now I have to ride into the Parc des Princes with a man stinking of Calvados, in last place. Henri warned us that there would be a crowd. 300,000 he said (the Velodrome doesn't fit that many). 300,000 people; waiting to see me come last.

Malakoff is that way. A simple turn around, I could go home. Cut keys. Do some welding at the bottom of the garden. Potter around in the shed, away from the madding crowds. Write a letter to Monsieur Persiaux accepting his job offer. See my wife and my son.

One last humiliation.

A wall of sound greets us as we enter the velodrome, shouts of "Cri-Cri we love you", flowers thrown onto the track; another thing to bring me to the floor. Duboc sprints, I follow. Get his wheel, Eugène, get his wheel – don't give them the pleasure of seeing you fail again.

Round the first turn, Duboc is faster than I gave him credit. I can't hold his wheel.

The back straight, I'm catching him, I have his wheel. He looks round – that's fatal. I attack and he finds extra, round the last bank we go. Duboc panting and grunting – undignified – why am I doing this? Why am I trying? What's the fucking point. I let up, Duboc celebrates – celebrates what, coming second-last on the day?

Some riders are pathetic.

I can't see if I've crossed the line, the crowds are onto the track, and the tears in my eyes have blurred my vision anyway. Would I have received this reception if I had won? It's over. It's finally over. I lost like a man and it never hurt so bad.

There's no room to move, so I succumb to the crowd, my eyes streaming, my heart in my throat – the French love a loser, and they've got one now. Am I to be the much-loved, plucky but unlucky loser all my life? Twice now I've had the Tour in my hands, twice now I've lost for no reason of my own, and yet here I am, a hero to 300,000 people. It's stupid beyond belief.

Jean-boy is pulling me by the arm.

"We've got something for you, Cri-Cri," he insists. "We all pulled together – it's not much, but it's from us."

I look at the envelope, the money. "You shouldn't have done this, boys."

Lambot embraces me and looks me in the eye. "I'll never know if I'd have beaten you without the accident.

All I know is I'd rather have beaten you on equal terms."

I have no words. I just hold his shoulder and look down. And he does the same.

Desgrange grabs me by the arm and gives me that "I have no words" look, which he'll translate into 2,000 words for tomorrow's newspaper. He always finds a way.

And in this velodrome of 300,000 people, I am alone with my thoughts. Is there triumph in defeat? And for Lambot, is there defeat in triumph?

A rider deserves certainty, but what certainty can you get from a race where ill fortune can strike wherever she wants? What certainty can a rider ever hope for? That there's a sorceress lurking in every corner, waiting to push you off your bike or snap your forks, that there's injury and fatigue and hunger and pain, and if you don't face it like a man, there's humiliation in the paper the next day.

This is the Tour de France, the travelling shitshow put on by Henri Fucking Desgrange for the benefit of his newspaper, and it's just like it always was before the war. Pointless for the riders, but to these 300,000 people around me? It's life and death.

I look at Lambot, and I feel for the man. He's a formidable racer, but it's my fault he'll forever feel that his Tour was stolen, when the truth is, he rode the race of his life, and all anyone will talk about is how I lost the race. Or how I made all the money through coming second. So not only do I feel like crap that I lost the race on a technicality, I feel guilty because I ruined it for Lambot and took all the money.

Any kids wanting to be a cyclist, look away now. It's shit. A lifetime of shit. Forget it.

So now we're done. Time to go home. Shut the factory down. Another tour done and dusted. Pack the bike away, machine becomes man. Rider becomes civilian. I could get used to this lifestyle, even if it is just a few minutes old. I could open a bike shop, like Lambot. I could look after the garden, like Duboc. Or I could just smoke a pipe like Coomans and look back on my career. Perhaps Persiaux-Chardon is calling. A life in Raismes, opposite the station, welding and hammering and making things, being useful. I'll drink at the bar, hold up the zinc, sink a demi with the miners at lunchtime. The race is over, but I think the racing itself is over.

And what does a rider think of when the racing is over?

If he's any good, nothing.

Stage 15

1	Jean Alavoine (FRA)	15h 00' 54"
2	Luigi Lucotti (ITA)	s.t.
3	Honoré Barthélémy (FRA)	s.t.
4	Léon Scieur (BEL)	s.t.
5	Jacques Coomans (BEL)	s.t.
6	Jules Nempon (FRA)	+ 5' 02"
7	Firmin Lambot (BEL)	+ 10' 09"
8	Joseph Van Daele (BEL)	+ 11' 08"
9	Alfred Steux (BEL)	+ 34' 15"
10	Eugène Christophe (FRA)	+ 35' 47"

General Classification

1	Firmin Lambot (BEL)	231h 07' 15"
2	Jean Alavoine (FRA)	+ 1h 42' 54"
3	Eugène Christophe (FRA)	+ 2h 26' 31"
4	Léon Scieur (BEL)	+ 2h 52' 15"
5	Honoré Barthélémy (FRA)	+ 4h 14' 22"
6	Jacques Coomans (BEL)	+ 15h 21' 34"
7	Luigi Lucotti (ITA)	+ 16h 01' 12"
8	Joseph Van Daele (BEL)	+ 18h 23' 02"
9	Alfred Steux (BEL)	+ 20h 29' 01"
10	Jules Nempon (FRA)	+ 21h 44' 12"

EPILOGUE

Henri Desgrange

"Alphonse, dear boy, you reek of coffee."

He does, dear reader. Absolutely positively whiffs of it. He shuffles in his chair.

"When are the first riders arriving? Hm?"

Impatient, aren't you, Alphonse. Give them a chance.

I must update you, I suppose, for dear reader I am aware that the Tour is over and you are still here – as am I. It is the day after the final stage; Alphonse and I are ensconced in l'Auto's offices here on the Boulevard Montmartre, 9th arrondissement, 1st floor, corner office, and I must admit that I am feeling the first pangs of withdrawal; I am missing that rush of excitement at the prospect of a day's racing in the Alps or organising a checkpoint in the Landes. I'm missing the Brasier and the mountains.

Back to the eternal greyness of our capital, a grey city with grey buildings as high as the eye can see, and more often than not, a grey sky.

'Tis a typical Paris late summer's day. Musty warmth,

grey sky, the hope for rain hanging in the air, unfulfilled.

Ah, to be on the bicycle myself right now. To the Bois de Boulogne, out to Rambouillet, around the Yvelines, back in time for supper. One still has the legs, you know.

Alas, I am with Alphonse, a coffee-riddled, stress-filled little man who has – allow me to give him his dues – survived the last month (just about) and has got nine of his men – legally – to the finish line. And we await the riders for their final checks, a traditional "weigh-in", and a final interview before we set them free to wherever it is they came from.

Alphonse drums on the desk. How annoying.

"Alphonse, Alphonse, if you really must demonstrate your impatience, perhaps go outside and pace up and down the corridor, but don't drum on the desk like an impertinent child."

Our boredom is punctuated by a clutter from outside. Two riders stumble through the office with their bikes, ah it's the boys from Belgium, Léon Scieur and our Tour winner, Firmin Lambot. Alphonse embraces them both; I extend my hand in congratulations.

"Firmin, our valiant Firmin, and Léon the Locomotive!"

They nod, and I can't help feeling that Lambot is less than comfortable with the situation. It can't help that the nation has fallen in love with Christophe.

"A few words, and then we'll get down to the formalities," I offer. "Firmin, Firmin, many congratulations, my dear boy, you have done yourself proud – and your nation I may venture – how are you feeling today?"

He has such sad eyes, like an animal about to be eaten. Doesn't look like a Tour winner when he's in his civvies.

"I'm fresh a daisy, Monsieur Desgrange. Fresh as a daisy and over the moon!"

Ah Firmin, I know when a rider is lying to me. It's

usually when they move their lips. They're disappointed, they're angry, they're feeling down, but they don't want me to know, because I'm Henri Desgrange, the man with the iron fist, the man who held the hour record, the man who fought the Germans at the age of 50.

They don't want to appear meek, but I wish they would.

I move to reassure him. "Firmin, you're a deserving winner of this Tour, I hope you realise that. And when you're old and retired, and you look back on this race, remember the tenacity with which you fought, remember the attacks you launched on Christophe, on Pélissier, on the rest of the field, and remember how absolutely nobody could keep up with you on stage 14, remember that."

"Yeah Dejo," shouts Léon from across the room, where Alphonse is weighing him while checking the bike. "That's what I said."

He looks right back at me. "That's what I keep telling myself, sir."

"And you keep telling yourself until the day you die, Firmin Lambot. You've done yourself proud."

I turn to Léon. "And you, dear boy. A future Tour winner if you carry on like that!"

He smiles. "Thank you, Mr Desgrange, that means a lot to me."

"You just need a bit more in the mountains and you'll be up there with the best of them."

Signatures and paperwork sorted, we shake hands, and the boys disappear down the stairs, clunking their bikes along with them.

I watch them from the window as they wheel their bikes down the Boulevard Montmartre, now just two Belgians from a nowhere town called Florennes, caps pulled down over one ear, children chasing after them.

"Do you think he deserved it, Alphonse?" I cry out,

keeping my gaze on the Boulevard.

He mumbles something non-committal.

Of course he bloody deserved it.

He deserved it for every minute he spent a prisoner of the filthy Prussians, for every day he went hungry in Antwerp while waiting for the Allies to break through the lines and come to his rescue. It must have felt like a lifetime.

He deserved it on behalf of every rider who died in the war, for every rider who made it to the start line, for every rider who made it to the finish. He deserved it for turning up with so little training in his legs and for feeling his way into the race. Ah, at last, a rider who could achieve such a feat. He deserved it for the sheer, ravaging beauty of those attacks against Pélissier and Christophe, for the unrelenting audacity of hoping that one of his attacks would stick, and stick they did, in the end.

And here's the thing we will never say out loud, nor in print – he deserved it because his bike held. Ah – the bike. We speak so much of the man, the athlete, but what of the machine powered by those legs? How can it be that one man's forks break twice in the space of three Tours while another man's forks hold firm? He blames the witch, but that's a superstition that arises only through failure. You don't find a Tour winner transported to the line by magic fairies; you don't find a stage winner thanking the goblins and the pixies!

A witch, indeed. Modern riders have a multitude of excuses for ill fortune.

What more apt winner could there be, then? As France and Europe stand in the rubble of our nightmares, Firmin Lambot shows us that revival is possible, with determination and hard work, perseverance and just that little bit of good fortune.

The Tour, perhaps, owes Firmin Lambot something of a debt. And perhaps, I muse, we shall take the Tour one day to Florennes, as a mark of respect. Pay our dues.

Perhaps we shall do that.

AFTERWORD

I lose track of why I chose to write about this particular Tour. I started so long ago, it's starting to pass into mythology. Did I choose it because it was ignored by other writers? Or because it was so cruel? Or did I just think it would make a good story?

Whatever, I decided very early on I didn't want to write a blow-by-blow history of the race. I'd rather leave that to the Tour historians like Les Woodward who do a much better job than I ever would. And besides, it's so hard to relate to these early Tours. It's far easier to relate to the Coppis and the Bartalis, the Merckxes and the Hinaults… but Lambot, Christophe and Alavoine? If you read some books, you'd believe that road cycling only really took off after the second World War.

What I wanted to do was bring this Tour – and this era – to life. After all, I thought, they're just blokes riding bikes. What's so different?

OK, there are some differences:
- These were pretty heavy bikes
- Some of the blokes had moustaches, although apparently it was going out of fashion (see Eugene Christophe)
- You only had one bike, and if it broke – you had to repair it yourself
- The roads were shot to pieces
- Many members of the peloton had been killed in the war
- Stages were sometimes over 430km long and started at 2 in the morning

OK, so it's quite different. But essentially, the riders are just blokes riding bikes. Even if the thought of riding 5,500km in 15 stages makes you shudder, imagine what it must be like starting at 2am, carrying out all your repairs yourself, and riding on gravel roads all day.

So, to bring this Tour to life, I needed to find the voices of the riders and the race organisers. Henri Desgrange is the most obvious – his florid prose is everywhere. There are records of Eugene Christophe, and Jean-Paul Rey's excellent biography forms the basis of much of Christophe's many malheurs, and I am extremely grateful to Jean-Paul Rey for this. It's an excellent book: Le Damne de la Route. If your French is any good, read it.

Henri Pelissier, too, is well-recorded, but riders such as Jean Alavoine, Honore Barthelemy and Firmin Lambot are less well covered. Barthelemy's voice in particular is cobbled together from a few interviews that I could find in L'Auto, while I admit that I completely invented a voice for Maurice Machurey, the man in charge of getting the feeding station ready in Arromanches. But mostly, I have been as loyal to the riders whose voices I have stolen as possible.

So if I've had to make things up here and there for the likes of Machurey, the race itself is retold exactly as it happened. It is true that Henri Pelissier was attacked by the peloton on stage 4 down to Sables d'Olonnes when he stopped to tighten his headset, and it is true that he put in a heroic effort to haul them back. It is a fact that his brother went with the peloton, and it is also a fact that he was warned for relaying. However, I have no idea whether he took drugs or not that day – his admission that he (and other riders) were basically pharmacies on wheels was several years later, but I took the liberty of prescribing him some 'dynamite' for this stage, given the circumstances.

For the background and the voices of Firmin Lambot and Leon Scieur, I have to thank Jean-Pol Rayp and Erich Van Boven, whom I have never met in person, but with whom I have exchanged several emails. Erich had the fortune of knowing Leon Scieur in person, and provided me with a treasure trove of information on the two Belgian riders from the town of Florennes.

For further background, I'm extremely grateful to Dries de Zaeytijd at the Wielermuseum in Roeselare. Not only did he give me access to the museum's archives (which are extensive), Dries took the time to prepare the research for me, bookmarking relevant pages about the Belgian riders in particular, making the job even easier. While the archive isn't open to the public, the museum is and any road cyclist who wants to understand the rich history of cycling will make a pilgrimage to Roeselare.

Finally, this book would not be what it is without the editing and the wise counsel of James Spackman from Pursuit publishing. He took the time to read the first manuscript and provided me with direction – and has continued to advise throughout.

I imagine if you're reading this book that you're probably a cyclist. You probably spend the month of July in front of ITV4 wishing you could take three weeks off and follow the Tour. So if you are, then remember these are just blokes riding bikes. Just like you. And what you have just read did actually happen, and I think it's a story that deserves to be told. And hopefully, by now you'll think – as I do – that riders like Christophe, Lambot and Alavoine deserve to be mentioned in the same context as some of the great riders of more recent years.